Rising

Rising

How to Thrive as a Corporate Executive While Staying True to Yourself

Kelly Hopping

Published by Game Changer Publishing

Paperback ISBN: 978-1-961189-81-2
Hardcover ISBN: 978-1-961189-82-9
Digital: ISBN: 978-1-961189-83-6

GC GAME CHANGER PUBLISHING
www.GameChangerPublishing.com

DEDICATION

This book is dedicated to my husband, Jim, for supporting me unconditionally despite all my flaws, for loving the Lord with all his heart, and for leading our family with faith and humility.

For Jim - my love, my soulmate, my forever.

Rising

How to Thrive as a Corporate Executive

While Staying True to Yourself

Kelly Hopping

GC GAME CHANGER
PUBLISHING

www.GameChangerPublishing.com

Table of Contents

Introduction

Throughout my life, I have rarely strolled. I have moved with intent and purpose almost every moment of every day. I have never walked or even jogged on the hamster wheel of life. I have sprinted, full speed, from the moment I stepped out of bed every morning. I have tried not to waste time, opting instead to schedule almost every second of my day, allowing very little white space for thinking, reflecting, or breathing. I have booked meetings or commitments right up until the moment I needed to move to the next one. I have often just switched to my phone mid-meeting and taken the rest in the car, picked up my kids, put myself on mute long enough to tell them "Hello" and to be really quiet for a few minutes, and then drove them to their next activity while finishing up the call. Always a perpetual multitasker, I fold laundry while watching Netflix, play *Sudoku* while listening to a podcast, and read *People* magazine while using the bathroom. I have been on a continuous, never-ending mission to check boxes and accomplish every daily goal until I crash on the couch after the kids go to bed (or usually before).

As much as it pained me to admit, all of this was driven by my ego. I was always evaluating myself based on an artificial sense of self-esteem fueled by what I accomplished, not by who I was as a human. I would like to think that I have always been wide open and that I have trusted the process, but I have been more consumed with achieving the next great thing and over-delivering on other people's expectations of me. In reality, those unsustainable milestones were probably just mine. I created a narrative of judgment by the people around me that motivated me to make decisions based on what others might have thought. It was a vicious cycle of doing more to seek validation to power my own pride, which ultimately meant that I was never satisfied unless I was doing and succeeding. I wanted others to trust and believe that I could do anything I set my mind to because that is what I believed about myself.

I learned that busyness was the anchor I grabbed to satisfy the Achiever in me (both my #1 Gallup[1] strength and my Enneagram 3[2] profile type). Filling every second of the calendar gave me purpose, whether I was completing a project, attending a meeting, catching up with a colleague, or taking my daughter to volleyball practice. The idea of unfilled space was haunting me for years as I pushed for productivity every moment of the day. When I combined my achiever mindset and my need for affirmation with my top Gallup weakness (deliberation), I would make a series of very fast decisions, often based on what I could reasonably accomplish. I would take all the information that I had at that moment, consider all the pros and cons that were immediately obvious, process it quickly in my head and often out loud, and then make a decision and go. I was thoughtful and decisive but incredibly expeditious. I was too much of a planner and driver to let life happen to me, so I masterminded the outcome in short, intentional bursts. I prided myself on the ability to do all of this in a matter of minutes or hours, not days, weeks, or months. I wouldn't think about something too long before I had either acted on it or shut it down.

I called that efficiency, and it became my superpower. I multiplied my capacity through an efficient operating model to get a significant amount of work done in a short period of time. This became a highly productive way to make the most of my finite workday, balance time with my family, and accelerate my career. It usually put me in the driver's seat and protected me from failure.

---

[1] https://www.gallup.com/cliftonstrengths
[2] https://www.enneagraminstitute.com/type-3

But it was exhausting and unsustainable. I would wake up thinking about all the balls I had in the air, and if just one unplanned thing happened—a flat tire, a family emergency, a last-minute work trip—all the balls would tumble to the ground. Failure would be imminent. As my career and leadership position progressed, I realized that I needed space to think and dream, to lay out a vision for my team, and to reflect when things didn't go as planned. I also needed to re-evaluate my goals and be okay with falling short occasionally. As a mom, I wanted to be completely present with my kids, looking them straight in the eye and engaging in intentional conversation, not just hustling them through the logistics of childhood. And as a wife, I mourned the reduction in quality time sitting and talking with my husband about our family and real life, not just rushing to our next over-scheduled family commitment. I needed to pause.

Burnout is real, especially after a massive failure crushed my confidence and forced me to re-discover what mattered the most to me. So, in July 2021, after 20 years of working and progressing in my career at breakneck speed, I made the very difficult but necessary decision to take a 6-month sabbatical to refresh, recharge, and refocus. I left my company where I was the Chief Marketing Officer leading a team of 110 people, and then, rather than rush to the next gig—as every fiber of my being triggered me to do—I gave myself permission to breathe, reflect, and discover what the next chapter looked like. Failure creates opportunity, but I had to stop, drop, and listen to figure that out.

As a recovering control freak, people pleaser, and perpetual achiever, embracing a world of uncertainty was extremely uncomfortable for me. For the first time in my life, I created margin in my day and in my head to be present and open to where life took me. I took a minute to think, a minute to dream, a minute to reach out to a friend, and a minute to see a need and try to fill it. Before my sabbatical, every situation created an opportunity. However, I lost sight of those opportunities because I was either too slammed to notice or too exhausted to care. Just having space to be and taking the time to listen opened my eyes to so much more. Gratitude became a real-time instinct rather than an after-the-fact hindsight. By having time, I allowed myself to be real, to feel raw emotion, to forgive myself, and to respond genuinely. My sabbatical changed my life.

Sabbatical taught me to become very protective of my time, making sure that I am focusing my energy and hours on topics and causes that I am passionate about. By month three of my sabbatical, I was still running hard every day but getting comfortable with space in between to call a friend or read or take a nap. By the end of month four, I was finally, for the first time in my adult life, saying "no" to requests for my time and attention, feeling fulfilled by the things I was choosing to invest in and not missing the things I gave up.

I was proactive and reached out to people I wanted to learn from to discover new career ideas like entrepreneurship, consulting, venture capital, and private equity. I discovered that I liked owning something and having a community around me. I also learned that returning to a large company in a leadership position felt safe and stable, but not necessarily energizing and new, given my history. I didn't want to take a sabbatical to then transition right back into what I was doing before.

I learned a lot about myself during my extended time off. The need to feel busy will always be a motivator for me, but I now recognize that busyness is also a distraction from listening to where my heart is being pulled. I could fill every second of the day with "stuff" and miss out on the opportunities to serve, hang out with my family, spend time with a friend, or be spontaneous. Creating that margin allowed me to feel again, and in fact, I cried every single day during my sabbatical—not sobbing or tears of sadness, but just a crack in my voice or unexpected emotion when telling a story, watching a commercial, or praying for others. I had time and headspace to engage and respond to emotion.

I didn't have time before my sabbatical to feel with my whole heart. "Oh, your mom died? I'm so sorry to hear that. Gotta run to my next meeting. I'll pray for you." I would forget to check in with people to see how they were coping. I would forget to ask my husband about that big situation at work. I would forget to follow up with my parents on that personal issue they were experiencing. Taking time to listen and follow that nudge that God placed on my heart, rather than pushing it down and hiding it with meetings and projects, allowed me to connect with myself, my family, and my friends on a level that I missed under the mountain of calendar obligations.

I also discovered space to reflect on my life and my career, allowing me to recognize themes and lessons learned from the ups and downs along the way. We all step blindly from one moment to the next and pray that we are moving in the right direction, but until I looked backward at the entire journey, I couldn't appreciate how far I had come.

So, during my 6-month sabbatical, I decided to write it all down and capture what I learned, hoping to shine a light on what I wanted to do in the next chapter of my life. I needed to see where I stepped wisely and where I lost my footing. To be perfectly honest, I felt a little foolish writing this story. I have never experienced a traumatic childhood or a serious illness. I wasn't abused or homeless. I didn't grow up in a divorced household or live through real financial struggles. Instead, my journey was a spiritual and professional evolution through beautiful mountains and occasional valleys, but never from the view of rock bottom. I had a couple colossal failures that stopped me in my tracks, but their impact was manageable and life-giving in the grand scheme. I can't pretend to relate to what others have been through, but I know what my experience has been.

As a Harvard Business School graduate, an experienced Chief Marketing Officer, a wife to the love of my life, and a mother of three active children, I have benefited greatly from mastery of the proverbial rat race. My accomplishments have fueled my confidence, and I perceived my own value to be based on what I did, not who I was. Grounded in family values and growing in my Christian faith, my need to never disappoint others often resulted in letting myself down. Exhaustion and burnout left me grasping for the fast, easy answer, but time and reflection allowed me to be present, lean into the margins, take a hot minute to think, and gain clarity on where I am meant to be. I have learned that when you're traveling at full speed, the step off the treadmill can be a bumpy fall. For a long time, the anticipation of that fall made me think it was easier to just stay on and keep pushing.

Over time, however, and with a lot of patience, the Lord changed my heart and showed me that I had to let go of my own need to control, plan, and impress. I had to learn to trust the road that He laid out for me. My journey illustrates a personal and professional evolution: from always doing what was expected of me and fighting to control the outcome, to being open to where life takes me by trusting in God's plan. Finding my purpose in this way brought the ultimate freedom and joy that strictly pleasing others or seeking their approval will never satisfy.

I don't share my journey to preach or dictate how others should do it, nor do I expect empathy for my perfectly imperfect life. I am a sample size of one, so this is by no means fact, but I only open my heart as a way of sharing how I was affected, what gave me hope along the way, and what I learned from all of it. If the Lord takes me home tomorrow and I don't get the chance to share everything I have gleaned from this world with the people and community I love, then I have missed the opportunity to connect with others through my story. If nothing else, I hope my kids will get the chance to know a little more about their mom, and maybe some young, hungry future leader will have a smoother ride to the boardroom (or at least have an excuse to get the heck out of corporate).

Every day, I learn, grow, and gain perspective—emotionally, profession-ally, and mentally—desperately trying to rise above the noise, above my own artificial limitations, and above the unrealistic, self-imposed expectations of perfection. I am nowhere near the peak, nor do I think I will ever fully get there, but I am *rising*.

This is my story, a tale of resilience and empowerment as a corporate executive trying to stay true to myself along the way. This is a love letter to my husband, my children, my parents, my friends, my mentors, my colleagues, and the leaders in my life who believed in me and brought me along for the ride.

PART 1

The Road to Sabbatical

CHAPTER 1

Failure Was Not an Option.

I once tried to quickly describe my friend Reese to my husband Jim before they met. This is a difficult thing to do in a few short words. However, I said, "He wears pleated pants, probably." Immediately, my husband had a clear picture—nice guy, trustworthy, not trendy, classic, consistent. Sometimes those nuggets give us more insight into someone's character than a list of demographics or work history. So, before I start this story, let me tell you a little about the "pleated pants" elements of my life.

I think that *Pitch Perfect* is one of the greatest movies ever made. While I'm at it, I prefer *Grease 2* over the original *Grease*. I like Anna better than Elsa because I prefer interesting, unique, intelligent, and funny. I think the prince would be bored of Elsa in a year. I am an incredible sleeper. I don't sleep until noon or waste my days away sleeping, but when I hit the pillow at night, I fall asleep in seconds and often wake up eight hours later in the exact same position. If I have a 20-minute break during the day, I will sleep hard for at least 19 minutes. Sleep might be my number one strength.

I think that Young Adult (YA) and Historical Fiction novels are the best genres of literature. YA books are the only ones that represent true, raw emotion, not jaded yet by real life. In addition, my favorite movies are the ones based on books I have read. Most people think that "the movies are never as good as the books," but that's the point. If I have read the book, the movie doesn't have to be as good because I can fill in the blanks in my mind. That's why I read.

I think that either cheese, avocado, or peanut butter can make any food taste better (but not all at the same time). I have an unnatural phobia of wet paper, Band-Aids, and anything sticky, and I get completely distracted by missed belt loops. I can ask new people one question and decide immediately if we're going to be friends or just acquaintances: "Do you prefer Saturday football or Sunday football?" There is only one right answer. If they add Friday night football to the mix, then we are destined to be soul mates.

I believe that in the absence of intimate personal knowledge, brands are a surrogate for quality. People aren't necessarily brand snobs. They are deciding based on what they've heard versus what they actually know from experience. That includes our own personal brands, so we must make good choices.

I think that the number one problem with people today is that no one takes responsibility for their actions. Everyone wants to blame someone else, yet the easiest way to learn, improve, and forgive is to just say, "Yep, I screwed up. I'm sorry." An apology is the fastest way to disarm a situation.

I am not typically a crier, but my voice cracks when I speak publicly sometimes, making me sound more emotional than I really am. Maybe stating my feelings out loud brings them to life for me, highlighting a deeper issue that I am not aware of. I never do the same thing twice if I can avoid it. With time being a limited resource, I want to use my precious moments to do something new—watch a new show (not a rerun), eat at a new restaurant (not a neighborhood favorite), or travel to a new place on vacation. Watercolor, Florida, is my one exception.

I believe the next great Broadway show should be a musical based on the entire Styx collection. The thought of a "Come Sail Away" solo starting slow and escalating into a dynamic group dance number leading into Intermission sounds like the perfect theater experience to me.

And finally, I believe in Jesus Christ as my Lord and Savior, and I trust every word of the Bible as truth.

I believe that I was saved by faith based on no act of my own but only by the incredible grace and mercy of God.

I have witnessed the daily blessings of Jesus in every part of my life, and I know without question that He is in charge, that He loves me, that He does not waste suffering, and that He has a purpose for everything in my life. God is so good.

So now that I have shared a little about who I am, I'll go one step further. I don't fail. I have always refused to fail. I have subconsciously engineered my entire life to avoid any risk of failing. To me, failing has always been a sign of weakness, a lack of preparation, or a loss of control. Failure happened to people who weren't driven enough or who weren't focused enough on the end result to push through every reasonable obstacle to achieve success. I believed that I could will anything into being if I just wanted it badly enough and was willing to take the steps to make it happen. Don't get me wrong. I was never willing to compromise my integrity to win at all costs, but I was naïve enough to believe that there was always a reasonable, moral path to avoid failure. It never crossed my mind that I couldn't have it all or that anything I desired was out of my reach.

Growing up, I couldn't visualize my career or what I wanted to do with my life. Sure, I would imagine being all the things talked about in children's books—a doctor, a lawyer, a teacher—but I never actually pictured what it would look like to make one of those careers happen. Rather, I pursued achievement and competence in everything I did—school, sports, student government, whatever. I found joy in being overly competent at most things, but I didn't love any one thing enough to pursue it wholeheartedly. I liked playing all the sports, not going all out on one. I loved to go water skiing and snow skiing every year or two, just to confirm that I could still get up and do it gracefully. I have always played golf at least once a year, not because I am trying to lower my score, but because I wanted to assure myself that I was good enough to play with anyone without making a fool of myself. I didn't need to be the best at everything. I just needed to know that I could do everything well enough to hang with the best of them. That drive made me very successful and well-rounded, but it also ensured that I wouldn't fail miserably. As a pleaser, I always liked accolades and affirmation from the people around me.

That's why I chose engineering—not because I wanted to build beautiful new designs and change the world, but because I was good at math and science. It wasn't about finding something I loved; it was about doubling down on my strengths so that I could be successful at it. I believed competence would lead to passion, not the other way around. And I believed capability was the best first step toward accomplishment and satisfaction.

In some ways, it can be. It's hard to imagine a dream without some understanding of the skills needed to pursue that dream. To me, that list of "skills" was functional—math, science, problem-solving. The challenge in that approach is that it limits imagination to what is known and what can be visualized versus the journey of discovering what could be. It limits capabilities to a predefined list, restricted by knowledge and proficiency of academic competencies and experiences. Although I was not a visionary for this ultimate life destination, I always anticipated my next step. It was one foot in front of the other, focused on the next big milestone. From success in high school to my admission to Texas A&M University, to graduating with honors in engineering—it all happened right on track. My career was my next step, and I knew that whatever first job I took based on whichever recruiters came to campus would define my career path. If they were providing benefits and matching 50 cents on the dollar for my 401K, then it would be a good job.

Ironically, I had always been allowed to dream as big as I wanted because I had been blessed beyond measure while growing up, with no limiting circumstances or cynical perspectives to hold me back. But I didn't dream big. Instead, my plans were practical. I focused on what I believed was expected of me on the stair-step path I'd carved out for myself. It wasn't about what I wanted to do, but rather what I thought I was supposed to do.

I also never imagined having to choose or make trade-offs between work and family. I just always believed that I could have it all, whatever "all" was. I knew I would drive my kids to and from school and football practice every day. I knew I would cook dinner every night, put the kids to bed, and go to church on Sunday. I knew I would do great things at work, get promoted, and have enough money to pay for whatever I needed. I knew I could go out with my friends and have fun, but still come home to an adoring husband. And I knew my children and dog would be healthy and well-behaved. I just always knew that it would all work out as planned. Maybe I was naïve…

CHAPTER 2

Failure Happens Despite All the Best Intentions.

In 2021, despite all the learnings and blessings from more than 20 years of corporate experience across 15 different roles with consistent progression across six different companies, I experienced my greatest failure professionally. I failed at discernment in making a major career decision. I failed at choosing the right company. I failed at understanding culture, I failed at trusting my gut, I failed at prioritizing my non-negotiables, I failed at protecting my team, and I failed at making the impact I wanted to make.

Up until that point, I had been very fortunate in my career, driven by incredible mentors who were always in my corner. I discovered a pattern after 20 years that I had not applied for a job since college. Every opportunity that came my way had been the result of an advocate who recognized the potential in me and took me along for the ride. They either recruited me, recommended me, or partnered with me to open invisible doors that I would have never known existed without these promoters pursuing me and exposing me to growth opportunities.

Let me go back to when my failure began. Nine months earlier, in October 2020, while serving Gartner as the Chief Marketing Officer in their Digital Markets division, my friend Christy from Rackspace, where we both previously worked, called about a CMO position at her new company. Although I was flattered, I was happy at Gartner and told her that I was not interested, but that I would send her some names of great candidates that I did recommend. The opportunity was an "ivory tower" CMO role, which is how I refer to brand and communications leadership roles. Growth marketing and demand generation were not included, and I felt that my ability to impact the company's market position would be hindered significantly if my influence stopped at the top of the funnel. Christy asked if I would at least speak to the Executive Recruiter and share my thoughts on the scope of the position. I met with him, had a fantastic conversation, and he recommended that I speak to the hiring manager, the founder and CEO, directly about how I would approach marketing at his company.

I met with the CEO (we'll call him "Tom") over Zoom while on vacation in Marble Falls during Thanksgiving. We were supposed to meet for an hour and ended up continuing for 2-½ hours. On one hand, I was flattered that Tom was willing to spend so much time with me and then recommend that I meet with the next executive in line; on the other, I realized that in this "interview," I said approximately three sentences. He spoke the rest of the time. Although I appreciated the context and his perspective, the lack of interest in my background or experience over 150 minutes of discussion should have raised an alarm. This was my first red flag.

Over the next two months, as I dragged out the interview process week by week, I continued to meet with the rest of the leadership team. The role was eventually expanded to include all of marketing, from brand to demand, which helped pique my interest more. Everyone was extremely kind, relatable, and complimentary of the company's growth trajectory. However, every single executive mentioned, as if I should know already, that I would "get used to Tom" over time. Or they would imply a consistent theme about the extreme hub and spoke model of the company where every decision, even the most tactical, must go back to the Tom hub for approval. That was my second red flag.

Regardless, I was winning rave reviews from the interviewers, according to the recruiter, which of course, my "words of affirmation" love language appreciated. However, I still made it clear consistently that I loved my current job at Gartner, and I really had no intention of leaving.

The country was still somewhat in lockdown due to the COVID-19 pandemic, so in parallel, Gartner was discussing the return to a full 5-day workweek in the office, and the thought of commuting again scared me. Despite the pain that COVID-19 caused many families around the world, I had selfishly fallen in love with the slower pace that came with quarantine, virtual work, and being with my family more. I was able to rest in the comfort and security of my own home with my favorite people on the planet while still engaging with the world through work and our Austin community, which sprung back to action within a couple of months after the lockdown. I could work right up until the moment I needed to transition to Mommy Uber without the addition of a 45-minute commute from downtown. I built a highly efficient, integrated machine for managing all the daily commitments and needs for both work and family in a flexible format over a 24-hour period, not compartmentalized cleanly between an 8-hour workday and the "all other" in the after-hours. I was unnerved at the potential loss of control and freedom to manage my workload in my own way. In short, I was not ready to go back to the office.

At the end of January 2021, Tom made me an offer to join the company as their Chief Marketing Officer. It was a Level 1 position, meaning that I would report to the CEO for the first time in my career, finally having the opportunity to really influence the direction of the company. The company was 100% remote, and they were extremely generous with compensation (almost twice what I was making at Gartner), offering a chance to accelerate growth in a hot market with all the resources and headcount I needed. My team of 100-plus marketers would be equal in size to my team at Gartner, and it was a newer, younger, but still substantial, private company growing at a faster pace than Gartner. Given my history of working for large, publicly traded companies, I became intrigued by the idea of working at home permanently and being a part of a rocket ship. Despite the compensation perks, there was no equity available in the company, even at this early stage. That was my third red flag.

After I received the offer, I asked to meet with the CEO again to talk about critical details like what success looked like and how we would work together. The recruiter told me, "No." He said that any questions I had for Tom, I could just ask him, and he would either give me his point of view or chase down the answer. That was my fourth red flag. In hindsight, I realized that the recruiter knew that another conversation with Tom would have ended in me declining the offer. I would have discovered through that conversation that Tom and I were like oil and water, doomed to butt heads from the very beginning. But because of my internal need to be affirmed and liked, I accepted the recruiter's answer. No one ever wants to be the high-maintenance candidate who brings drama before joining the company. What a mistake it was to sacrifice my own comfort with the job to save the recruiter from an uncomfortable task and Tom from an extra conversation.

I then asked about general corporate governance like a board of directors, advisory board, outside investors and stakeholders, equity partners, etc., but the company had none of those. Tom believed that outside voices cluttered decision-making. In other words, the founder was greedy and close-minded, unwilling to share the wealth or take feedback from experienced professionals who did this before. This was red flag number five. Did I mention that the CEO was at least 10 years younger than me and had never worked anywhere else, yet somehow believed that his view was the best and only way to drive the company?

I struggled with the decision for a couple of weeks, torn between taking a chance on something new or trusting my gut that told me to run fast the other way. I reached out to two of my CMO friends and mentors and walked them through the situation. On paper, this opportunity seemed like a fantastic offer—remote, significant compensation increase, large team, high growth company, reporting directly to the CEO—but they could hear the hesitation in my voice. I could not articulate the pit in my stomach that was blinking bright red with warning signs. Both gave me the same advice. "What's the worst that could happen? If you hate it, stay for a year, and then take a year off." With the increase in salary, that sounded reasonable and appealing. I prayed about it for days, and that feeling in my gut never subsided. Ultimately, I betrayed everything I was feeling and ignored every red flag, and I accepted the job anyway. The achiever in me, overflowing with positivity and WOO (winning others over), believed I could be the savior who came in, developed my team, and transformed the culture of the company through my leadership and charming personality. Unfortunately, that was not the case this time.

I have learned that sometimes we make career decisions based on a fancy job title, bigger scope of responsibility, or higher compensation. Sometimes we are more worried about flexibility and remote work. Oftentimes, we are concerned about what other people will think about our impressive new job and how many likes or comments we'll get when we get to update our LinkedIn status. Maybe we have fallen into the trap of defining success based on how the world views it versus what truly makes us happy and gives us purpose. Maybe we stay at a company too long for fear of the dreaded gap in the timeline on our LinkedIn profile. Maybe we don't have the confidence to leave an organization when we see the signs of danger because we see resignation as failure. Maybe any or all these things cause us to ignore red flags that are staring us in the face as we joyfully accept that new position.

Red flags are defined as any warning signs of danger ahead, but they often manifest as a feeling in your gut that something is just not right. In my experience, a toxic work environment is usually the product of a combination of red flags such as micromanagement, over-inflated communications, a lack of transparency, verbal abuse and never-ending criticism, high turnover, a lack of respect for your work-life balance, or a leadership team of "yes" people who don't have the backbone to say "no" or push back on the less-than-qualified boss.

A few weeks later, I had an awkward, uncomfortable conversation with my boss, Ken, at Gartner to let him know that I was leaving. I had been there two years and had developed a close, trusting friendship with him, so the thought of giving him the news ate at me for weeks. I assumed that the thought of having to resign was causing my anxiety and that once it was out, I would feel relieved. That relief never came, and the pit in my stomach never dissolved. I don't think Ken even believed that I was totally bought in on my decision. I know that he could sense a lack of conviction in my voice. I now believe it was the Lord trying to get my attention and save me from my own greed and earthly desires as I moved forward with the transition.

My first day on the new job, I watched Tom blast one of my teammates for 30 minutes for asking a question in a staff meeting. I then listened to him publicly shame one of the junior leaders on my team in front of 75 people. Then I started receiving multiple complaints from my boss daily where he would demand an impromptu Zoom call to explode over anything that he believed would affect his precious brand, like the size of the font on a social media post or the job title of a guest on our podcast.

For example, if we posted a generous and flattering customer testimonial from a happy customer, but it wasn't a C-level executive from a Fortune 500 company, he would command us to remove it immediately because it made him feel small. Or if an employee posted something from their own personal social media account that was even slightly political, like Happy Breast Cancer Awareness or Happy Juneteenth, he would scream at me for 20 minutes and then tell me to fire them. I noticed that everyone tiptoed through their jobs, not sharing their ideas or doing their best, most creative work. It became increasingly clear that I had joined a culture dominated by fear—fear of saying the wrong thing, fear of expressing an opinion, fear of retaliation. The meetings with my team shifted very quickly to how not to get yelled at rather than about how to grow the business. When I would interview candidates to join my team, I couldn't even try to sell them on the role with a straight face. I couldn't live with myself knowing that they might quit their other job to come to this company and later resent me for it.

After a few months on the job, in retrospect, I could very clearly recognize those red flags I tried to ignore in favor of money, title, and flexibility. Upon reflection, I have learned that I should never make a decision in a vacuum. That finite set of data points presented to me by a potential employer is not my only resource for decision-making. I have a lifetime of experience, an understanding of people and culture, and I have the power to ask a lot of questions and double-click into areas that seem fishy. That is my right as a candidate.

Despite an incredible team of marketers that I had the joy of leading, I only lasted at the company for a few months. It was my shortest job ever, but I learned very quickly that I was not the right "culture" fit. I was able to transform the organizational structure, rebuild the operating model, and drive a new strategy, but outside of my marketing bubble, I failed in every way. I thought that our job as executives was to add strategic value and help grow the company, but I soon learned that my job was to be a "yes (wo)man" and do what Tom said, whether I agreed or not. I thought I could live with the fact that it was founder-led with no advisory board, no board of directors, and no outside investors. I quickly realized that this structure fostered an intense culture of anxiety and did not empower me or my team to bring our whole selves to work every day.

I believed that a key objective as a Chief Marketing Officer was to help grow and enhance the brand, but I learned that when the founder equates his brand with the company brand, then the CMO might as well be wearing handcuffs. I hoped that by Tom hiring experienced senior executives, he would value our opinions on best practices within our function, but I discovered that my perspective and feedback were not welcome. Any opinion that varied from Tom's resulted in public shaming, reprimanding, and humiliation, fueled by his narcissistic need for validation. He would question our loyalty to the company in front of hundreds of people on a video conference if we shared any data point that might raise doubt about his perfect organization.

One example of this toxic culture was in the form of employee feedback. This company conducted employee engagement surveys every two months. Beyond the ridiculous frequency (every six months is standard), they were mandatory, and they only had two questions:

On a scale of 1 to 10:

1. How happy are you working here?
2. How likely are you to recommend this company to a friend?

The Chief HR Officer (CHRO) would go through the employee list and contact individuals who hadn't completed the survey to ensure we had 100 percent compliance. Other than the fact that that was an incredible waste of time and money for a CHRO, the survey responses were also not anonymous. No healthy company that actually values authentic feedback requires employees to identify themselves in their surveys. Imagine if you were working in an organization dominated by fear where you must do a survey every two months and everyone in leadership will know exactly how happy (or unhappy) you are. Would you be honest on the survey?

In my first pulse survey after a month at the company, I chose to be honest, giving the company a 5 out of 10 on both happiness and willingness to refer the company to a friend. I immediately received a call from the CHRO. In most healthy companies, the call would be made from concern that I was so unhappy as a new senior leader who managed a large team. An organization should be striving for engaged, happy employees and leaders, so I expected something along the lines of "I was bothered by your survey feedback. I would love to understand what we can do to make this company better. We want our leaders to be happy as that trickles down to the teams below. Would you be willing to share some examples of your experience?"

Instead, my call went more like this:

"I saw your survey results. Tom is not going to be happy. Are you sure you don't want to change your scores so that he doesn't get upset? We have an annual goal of keeping employee engagement above a 9, and your feedback is undermining that goal."

My jaw dropped, and I knew immediately that I made a horrible mistake coming to work at a company like this. They had no interest in a positive work environment. The CEO was so worried about creating an image of his company as a happy, engaged place of employment that he was using coercion and fear of retaliation to achieve that image.

I didn't change my answers.

In July, after only five months on the job and ongoing daily Slack messages from my boss criticizing every piece of content, every blog, and every web page my team created, I suggested that Tom should fire me. I said that I fundamentally disagreed with 90% of what he asked me to do because it was just bad marketing. I suggested that he hire a $70,000-a-year project manager to execute all his marketing whims. I told him that as a steward of the company's resources, I believed that paying me was a complete waste of money if he wasn't going to let me do my job. I promised that I would not quit, that I would not abandon my team, and that I would push through and salvage whatever I could to help grow the company, but it was in his and my best interests to fire me. A week later, the Chief People Officer called to tell me that Tom was letting me go. He did not even have the courage to tell me himself.

I felt shocked, yet relieved. My ego took a gut punch, even though I asked for it. I was caught between blaming Tom and feeling like a failure that I could not win him over. I failed at choosing the right opportunity. I failed at paying attention to red flags and trusting my own gut, letting earthly success, money, and power lure me away instead. I failed at managing up effectively, driving change in the culture, and influencing my boss positively. I failed at protecting my team from the abuse and humiliation at the hands of the CEO. I tried to stand up for them, but I was just incorporated into the same public disgrace right along with my team. I failed to bring my full self to work every day for fear of persecution. I did not like who I was in that organization. I don't quit anything I start, but I failed to finish the job that I was hired to do.

Not only did I fail, but I felt like a failure. I had to get over the shame and guilt of being "fired" for the first time in my career, even though it was my idea. When I asked to be fired, I thought he would fight for me, even though I knew that I wouldn't change my mind. He didn't fight. I honestly didn't care what he thought of me, but my need for affirmation was not used to being rejected. He was happy to just let me walk away… and that hurt.

CHAPTER 3

Failure Creates Space for Reflection.

Once I was done feeling sorry for myself and was able to lift my head up from what happened, I could finally breathe a huge sigh of relief for the first time in 5 months. My kids were away at an overnight camp that week, so I had five days of wrapping my arms around what I experienced and figuring out what the heck I was going to do next. I would sit on the couch and stare mindlessly at the TV. I would start conversations with my husband mid-thought as I was trying to process on my own and then blurting out my perceptions and feelings with no context. I prayed for clarity and peace about my new situation. *What was God teaching me? Where was He leading me? What did He have in store for me that I could not even fathom yet?*

This time forced me to think about why I took the job in the first place, given how much I loved my job at Gartner and how many glaring concerns I witnessed during the interview process. I think there was a part of me that loved being sought after. The idea that Christy, whom I respected, came to me with the opportunity was a huge compliment, and I believe that my ever-present need for affirmation and man's approval overshadowed my interest in the job or the company. Regardless of the reasons, God was teaching me something.

Stepping back from the situation and giving myself time to reflect revealed to me that I compromised who I was and what I knew was right rather than trusting my gut. I didn't need to ignore that pit in my stomach for some resume-builder or as a means of proving that I can do it. I see now that it's okay to say "no" to the opportunities that look good on paper, but that gave me pause and unease when thinking about the daily reality of working in that environment or with that leader. I can trust my own intuition. I know myself better than anyone else, and I needed to believe in that.

We left on vacation to Lake Tahoe the following week. On the flight, I discovered a resource called Above Board that focuses on executive opportunities for women and minorities, and I sent a couple of messages to some executive recruiters to let them know that I was looking. I felt this urgency to go back to work immediately for fear of that dreaded gap on my LinkedIn profile, even though I had a nice severance that would carry me for a while. As a high-achieving Harvard graduate and a former CMO at Gartner who has always been successful, I just could not fathom being "unemployed."

I enjoyed Tahoe for the week with my family, and when I returned to Austin, I had seven CMO interviews on the calendar. I immediately knew that the market was fine. I did not need to rush because the Great Resignation following COVID-19 left companies desperate for high-quality talent. The companies ranged from large, public technology companies to small, Venture Capital-backed start-ups and everything in between. I was impressed by the caliber of opportunities, and I was intrigued by the prospect of making an impact on these organizations. They were cutting edge, had strong product-market fit, and were highly relevant in their space. But I couldn't get excited. I dragged my feet on the second round of interviews because the thought of sitting through a lengthy hiring process or onboarding at a new company felt draining. I should have been well-rested after a week of lake life, but I was mentally and emotionally exhausted.

I started to grapple with this idea of taking a little more time off. First, it was, *Maybe I'll wait until the kids go back to school.* Then it was, *Maybe I'll wait until the medical benefits from my severance run out.* The thought of taking extended time away from work just felt too out of character for me. I was still reeling from a bit of humiliation and fury associated with the exit from my company, but it didn't compare to the energy block that kept me from wanting to go back to work. I mentioned all of this to my friend Megan who is also an Austin-based CMO in the technology sector. She recommended that I listen to a podcast that she just recorded for DemandGen Radio called *Managing Burnout: An Open Discussion on Balancing Your Career and Your Life.* Megan and I have kids the same age, and she took a 6-month sabbatical between jobs a few years earlier. This podcast episode featured her journey up to, during, and after her sabbatical, and it was a game changer for me. It resonated with me on so many themes— exhaustion, craving more quality time with my family, the inability to turn work off and have a focused conversation with my children, and the never-ending feeling of always being on. I almost cried with relief as Megan put words to what I was feeling.

I was burned out. I just exited a situation where I was very clearly not the right fit, which left me feeling that I couldn't trust myself, that I didn't know how to make the right choices on my career path, and that I was obviously not cut out for founder-operated private companies. I had been building my toolbox of experience at large, publicly traded companies for my entire career, and I was afraid that I somehow lost my ability for hands-on marketing execution, replacing it with marketing strategy by PowerPoint while leading through change and transformation. Beautiful decks allowed me to tell the story that I wanted to share and inspired the followers that I needed to bring the dream into a reality, but PowerPoint is not marketing. It is a rallying cry to gain influencers. I could speak marketing all day long, crafting the perfect strategy and narrative, but I was so far removed from actually touching and feeling the marketing vehicles that I wondered if I still knew how to do it.

I needed a break to rest and reset and figure out who I was and what I wanted. The Lord drew me to Matthew 11:28-30 which says, *"Come to me, all you who are weary and burdened, and I will give you rest. Take my yoke upon you and learn from me, for I am gentle and humble in heart, and you will find rest for your souls. For my yoke is easy, and my burden is light."* God calls us to rest in Him, to let go of our worries, and to allow Him to carry that burden for us. My always-on achiever finally felt free to embrace that and just let it all go for a little while.

Except for two years at full-time business school and three maternity leaves, I had been working nonstop for twenty-two years. I never gave myself permission to take a break between jobs to soul-search or take stock of where I was and what I wanted to do with my life. Just like when I was younger, I just followed the bouncing ball to the next opportunity on the prescribed path. I prayed about the idea of taking a break for a few months, and I shared my desire with my husband. I knew he would be supportive, but I also understood that this would have some financial implications.

Now, the gift of God's oversight on all of this is not lost on me. Two things are really necessary to take time off: money and medical benefits. My husband had been self-employed for the past few years, so we had always relied on my benefits to cover our family. This would've been a huge obstacle in my ability to take time off if it weren't for the fact that, one month earlier, before I left my job, my husband accepted a position leading the In School Suspension (ISS) program at my kids' middle school while continuing to run his own business. I was skeptical about him taking the job at the time, but he felt God calling him to pour into these kids who needed a light in their lives and a strong male figure to support them in making better decisions. Who knew that a month later, we would need those medical benefits that came with his school-district employment? (Hint: It's a God thing.)

We had severance pay from my company exit and medical benefits from his job, but how would this work? Would I just appear unemployed for six months? Would I just leave the current company end date open until I transitioned into a new role? I realized again just how guilty I am of always worrying about what others might think. This was my life. I had to do what was best for me, my family, and my own emotional well-being. Jim and I prayed about it for a few days, and each day I woke up with more clarity and confidence in the decision to take a break.

Finally, on August 6, 2021, while sitting in the audience at the Global Leadership Summit, listening to Juliet Funt share insights from her new book *A Minute to Think,* I fell to my knees and prayed for the Lord to guide me through this journey. I immediately knew what I needed to do. I sent emails to each of the recruiters and CEOs I interviewed with over the past couple of weeks. I told them that I appreciated their time, but I would be pulling myself out of the interview process to take a much-needed rest and recharge break for six months. I wished them all the best of luck in their organization's success, and I told them that if they were still looking for a CMO in January, then to give me a call.

From there, I took control of the narrative. I wrote a long post on LinkedIn, sharing my story, exposing my exhaustion and need for purpose, and shining a light on the burnout that ambitious career professionals experience during the never-ending pursuit of worldly success and fulfillment. It was raw and vulnerable, and it resonated with my network. I then changed my job title to "Chief Sabbatical Officer" and described it as "temporary, but necessary." My sabbatical calendar filled up with three to four coffees or lunches a week with former colleagues, up-and-coming young professionals, mentors, friends, and strangers who were on a similar path. My story hit a nerve with people because we were all going through this working parent/aspiring executive progressive career path in a fast-paced, instant gratification, stay-ahead-of-the-curve professional game. A female C-level sharing her story of burnout and taking the time she needed to find margin, purpose, and gratitude made others feel less alone, and I welcomed that distinguished position with humility and responsibility. I frequently heard,

"I've never seen a female executive be so bold in her decision to take time off." Many were inspired to take their own extended time away, yielding a community of strong leaders sharing their stories.

But I was still learning too. I was figuring out this sabbatical and new perspective thing one day at a time, but I was blessed to have others on the walk with me. As I navigated my new normal as a temporary stay-at-home, non-working former executive mom, I reflected on my life, how my wiring impacted this journey, and how this moment was part of my purpose.

PART 2

Wired to Win

CHAPTER 4

The Desire for Achievement Starts Early.

I grew up the younger of two kids. My brother, Kevin, is three-and-a-half years older than I am and is my total opposite. He calls himself the recessive gene of the family with his red hair, green eyes, left-handedness, and startling contrast in disposition to the rest of us. He sees the world in a completely different way, always riding the train of counterculture in the opposite direction of progress. I, on the other hand, began my pursuit of achievement at a very young age. My ambition to earn good grades or make the A team in sports came from my determination to set an example as a leader and not to let anyone down (me included). I always did what was expected of me because I loved the satisfaction of a job well done and the feeling of my parents' pride in my accomplishments. I wanted to please them, and I was motivated by their words of affirmation and the boastful way they spoke about me to their friends. I never wanted to disappoint anyone in any way. Even as a kid, failure was never an option for me.

I often wondered if I focused too much on my parents' approval because I knew my brother was not leaning in that direction. It was as if I felt like I owed them a tidy, packaged, well-groomed offspring that they could be proud of, while my brother often took the path less traveled. I also realized that my parent-pleasing motivation is what kept me out of trouble throughout my adolescence. I had the voice and face of my father blinking in my head anytime I even considered a little teenage ruckus.

Ironically, I don't believe that any of this pressure to achieve actually came from my mom and dad. I was blessed from birth with incredibly generous and loving parents who poured into me and my brother. I think I was simply wired for praise. According to Gary Chapman's book, *The Five Love Languages*, my love language is words of affirmation. This means that I felt most loved when the people around me used words to encourage and validate me. That motivation was incredibly addictive as a smart, driven, high-performing daughter, friend, athlete, student, professional, wife, and mother. It meant that I often made decisions based on what was going to garner the most positive praise in the short term, not necessarily what was going to make me the happiest over the long term.

Still, my parents always had high expectations for me, not because there were any conditions associated with my performance, but because they knew my potential. They wanted the most for me because they came from so little. They often played the role of good cop bad cop, with my dad being the stern one and my mom coming through with the secret compassion and understanding afterward. If my dad was tough on me, my mom would often sneak into my room after I went to bed to assure me that Dad was just being protective or that Dad would always regret it if he didn't give his guidance before I made a big mistake.

We sat down together at the round family dinner table almost every night, and my dad would share financial wisdom with us. Some key lessons he taught us:

- Never finance a car if you can help it. It declines in value as soon as you drive it off the lot.
- Never spend more on a credit card than you can afford on a monthly basis. The interest will kill you.
- Choose whatever job you want, but make sure you can live within those means.

- Real estate is always a good investment. Buy rather than rent if you can.
- Always tithe to the church.
- Maximize your contribution to your 401K. Bonus if you can find a company that will match 50 cents on the dollar.
- You only lose money in the stock market if you sell. When the price drops, hang on to the stock (if you can) and wait for it to bounce back.
- Make sure you always have medical benefits. One health issue without insurance and you'll be in debt for life.

As I grew up, I began to notice that I was an interesting mix of both of my parents. I was always very sociable like my mom, but I leaned toward athletics like my dad, enjoying competition and teamwork. I excelled at math like both of my parents, but I loved it like my dad. My mom blessed me with the drive for academics, while my dad instilled a love for business and the art of the deal. I like to think that my dad influenced my head while my mom guided my heart, both of which made me exactly who I am today.

Sports were the backbone and constant of my childhood. I learned how to win with grace, lose with dignity, share success with others, be a supportive teammate, respect authority, and pursue perfection to achieve excellence. My character was shaped by the hours on the court, both practicing and playing. I once read a quote from an anonymous dad on why he was willing to pay so much money for sports for his kids. "I don't pay for sports," he said. "I pay for the opportunities that sports provide my kids to develop attributes that will serve them well throughout their lives and give them the opportunity to bless the lives of others. From what I have seen so far, I think it is a great investment!" Playing team sports was my first taste of bringing leadership to life.

One odd elementary school habit that I never grew out of was a strange obsession with typing. My computer teacher gave us floppy disks that we could take home to practice typing, focusing on both accuracy and speed. I practiced nonstop, often dreaming about "asdf" and "jkl;" where my fingers rested naturally on the keyboard. I began typing with my fingers at all hours of the day, transcribing manuscripts on my desk as the teacher talked or drumming the air with my fingers as I sprinted down the basketball court. (Apparently, my constant multitasking started early.) My parents and friends would tell me after the game that they could see me typing while I was playing. What they didn't know was that not only was I air-typing every word that I was hearing, but I was also sub-consciously re-typing every sentence with altered words in order to ensure that the sum of the letters in the sentence was always a multiple of four and bonus points if I used every finger.

For example, during Christmas, every time I heard the word "poinsettia," I would retype it with my fingers as "poinseta" because that had eight letters (a multiple of four) and used every finger once. I recognize now that I am a very strange duck as I still, to this day, type and re-write almost every word I hear. I like to think that I will somehow stave off both Alzheimer's and Arthritis later in life by keeping my mind sharp and my fingers moving.

I grew up a regular churchgoer and attended New Braunfels Presbyterian every Sunday. I loved going there because my family seemed to know everyone. Church, however, was a ritual to me, not an emotional, life-giving experience. The robotic liturgy of hymn, Lord's Prayer, Apostles Creed, Old Testament reading, hymn, New Testament reading, sermon, and closing hymn was just a countdown until noon, when we were finally free. I never understood the purpose and inspiration of weekly church services.

That is, until one evening in 8th grade when I was kidnapped from my house (with my parents' consent) by a team of teenagers in a full-size Greyhound bus. I was taken, along with a whole crew of my friends, down to the Civic Center, where I walked into this loud praise and worship experience. Hundreds of teenagers filled the massive room, raising their hands in the air and singing along to infectious praise songs. The energy was palpable, as if we were all jamming at a rock concert. Eventually, the music stopped, and an evangelist named Jay Strack walked on stage and changed my life.

That night, I heard the gospel more clearly than ever before. Jay didn't talk about Noah's Ark or David and Goliath, or even the birth of Jesus in a manger in Nazareth. That was what I was used to hearing at church. Instead, Jay shared that Jesus is the son of God, fully man and fully God, and He came to earth to save us from our sins. He lived the perfect, sinless life we all should live, yet died the death we all deserved. Jesus was crucified on the cross as the ultimate price for our salvation, and he rose three days later, wandering the earth for 40 days and revealing himself to over five hundred people (1 Corinthians 15:1-8). His death and resurrection provided the freedom to know that we are all sinners, that God loves us anyway, and that we are already forgiven for our sins—past, present, and future. I learned that night that I was created in God's perfect image (Genesis 1:27), that He knew me by name, and that He wanted a relationship with me.

On that winter evening in 1991, I invited Jesus into my life, asking Him to be my Lord and Savior. I was saved by grace alone through faith alone (Ephesians 2:8). I was a sinner (and still am), but I made a commitment to pursue a life of righteousness, loving God, and loving others well, despite any missteps and bad decisions along the way. I knew that I would never be alone again and that the Holy Spirit would be with me every moment from that day forward. Although I didn't quite know what that meant at the time, I knew in my heart that Jesus was pulling me to Him.

Over the next four years of high school and throughout the rest of my life, I had this newfound faith to ground me in every decision I made—from my dating life to parties, friendships to academics, marriage to career choices.

Through my involvement in Young Life and Fellowship of Christian Athletes as well as Christian summer camps like T Bar M and Frontier Ranch, I dug into scripture to learn about who Jesus was and made every effort to pursue a relationship with Him. That didn't mean that I locked myself in isolation away from sin. It meant that I loved the Lord, and I tried to love others well. I prayed that my heart would beat for the things God loves and hurt for the things that break His heart. My beliefs never wavered, and that faith has guided my purpose and my life ever since, even if my steps wandered off course a bit sometimes.

CHAPTER 5

Summer Jobs Taught Me Hard Work. College Taught Me About Leadership.

I loved my four years of high school, which read like a brochure for the ideal small-town childhood. I played sports year-round, served as a leader on the Student Council, ran Eunice the Unicorn up and down the field after touchdowns as a Unicorn Handler, won Scholastic Achievement in the New Braunfels Junior Miss program, and made my debut in a huge, ruffly white ball gown with a Texas bow at the Mid-Texas Symphony Debutante Ball.

Throughout high school, I set off in earnest down the path that my parents and I engineered for me. It was very simple: make great grades in high school, graduate toward the top of my class, go to a large, traditional university in Texas, live the ultimate college experience with lots of friends, football, and fun, get a degree that I could actually use, get engaged (because in the south, we know that the only viable place to find an ambitious Christian man is in college), and then get a job with a 401K and buy a house as soon as possible. I didn't resent that path, nor did I have any ill will toward it. I just never considered an alternative. The achiever in me was always pursuing the next milestone, always being responsible and taking the next dependable step.

I spent my summers working in the very lively tourist community of New Braunfels. My first job was at Schlitterbahn, the largest water park in the world, which happened to be in my hometown. I was 15 years old. Child labor laws allowed kids to work only four hours at a time and no more than twenty hours per week. I spent those limited hours on the SWAT team—Schlitterbahn Waste and Trash—picking up nasty debris and carrying tubes all over the park in the blazing Texas heat. I came home every night with a dark line down the back of my socks, which I affectionately called Schlitter-juice. It dripped out of the corners of the trash bags when I emptied them at the end of my shift. Disgusting! I hated the job, but I loved the independence that came with having cash in my pocket (minimum wage was $4.25/hour back then), and it taught me the value of a dollar. I would ask my dad if I could go to the movies with my friends, and he would say, "Is it worth 3 hours of Schlitter-juice?" It also opened the door to a promotion to lifeguarding at Schlitterbahn the next two summers.

When I turned 16 and could work normal hours, I also began bussing tables at The Grist Mill, the famous restaurant behind Gruene Hall where stars like George Strait, Garth Brooks, Willie Nelson, and Merle Haggard performed. I loved the live music, working with the servers, who were all college kids, getting tipped out by the waiters at the end of the night, and snagging hush puppies every time I walked through the kitchen. I moved on to waiting tables the following summer, and I learned very quickly how to be efficient. I optimized every step I took. On the way to take table 60's order, I'd drop off a ketchup bottle for table 48, refill table 53's iced tea, and leave extra napkins on table 55. It was about minimizing steps and maximizing impact to reap the highest rewards in tips. This approach has dictated my approach to every role in my career, making the most of every moment to drive the highest result as efficiently as possible. Waiting tables also gave me a backup plan. I made great money and learned very quickly that if this whole post-college professional career didn't work out, I could always go back to waiting tables. This planted a certain fearlessness in me that there was always a backup plan. Accepting the idea of the worst thing that can happen reminded me that it's not that bad.

In 1995, I graduated #3 in my high school class and gave the graduation address at the ceremony. Before moving to College Station to attend Texas A&M a few months later, I spent my last summer in New Braunfels renting tubes at Jerry's Rentals on the Guadalupe River and selling swimsuits at a retail store called The Boxcar. I was fortunate that my parents were paying for college, but I worked two jobs that summer to earn extra spending money. This allowed me some freedom to get settled in at school my freshman year before I started working again part-time as a sophomore. As soon as classes ended that year, I began training for my commercial driver's license (CDL) so that I could drive a 40-foot university school bus 12 hours a week on campus. Bus drivers worked 4-hour shifts, could flex around class schedules, and earned $12 per hour as compared to minimum wage of $4.75 per hour, so I jumped at the opportunity. I learned quickly that a unique skill set like a CDL commands a premium in the market. This nugget of insight has served me well as I have navigated my career. Similar to positioning a new product in the market, I concluded that I must carve out a compelling differentiation to set myself apart from the competition. But back then, its value was in giving me the means to enjoy college to the fullest. And, let's be honest, that meant playing with my friends and watching football most of the time.

High schoolers from small towns in Texas have no reason to look beyond the state of Texas for college. I loved everything about Texas A&M University and its traditions. I knew that I never wanted to go to any other school except Texas A&M, but I needed a backup plan, and the achiever in me liked feeling wanted. So, I applied to Baylor, Southern Methodist University (SMU), and Texas Christian University (TCU). That need for words of affirmation reared its ugly head as I wasted application fees just to know I was accepted and that I would receive scholarship money. (It was a waste of time, too, in the days before online applications. I remember the painstaking precision required to line up those paper applications in the typewriter perfectly, clicking each letter one by one to make sure that I didn't mess up, which would require me to use White Out and then line it up again.) That pursuit of validation has affected so many life choices: who I said yes to on a date, which jobs I pursued, and which offers I accepted.

I majored in Chemical Engineering for some bizarre reason that had something to do with liking math and chemistry. I could never actually picture myself working in a chemical plant or on a pipeline somewhere, but I didn't know any better in college, especially not my first couple of years. I just knew that I wanted to get the very best degree I could from Texas A&M, well known for its fantastic engineering program.

Although I graduated from high school with a GPA well over 4.0, I started my first semester at A&M with a 2.03 at midterm. I panicked. I had never even had a B before, and now I was barely passing. I was not about to tell my parents, but I was committed to spending the rest of the semester working on bringing my grades up. I had been studying all along, but I was not aware of how curves worked at this point, and none of the exams were adjusted for the curve by midterm. So, despite the 36 I'd made on my first chemistry test, I somehow got an A in the class. By the end of that first semester, I had a 3.92 with my only B—my first B ever—coming from a one-hour chemistry lab. I figured out then that I could handle this whole college thing.

I spent four and a half years in college, and I truly had the time of my life. I approached college with the attitude that I wanted to meet as many people as possible, become the very best leader I could through organizations around campus, and find an interesting and well-paying job after graduation. Despite my desire to graduate in the top 1% of my class for high school, I wasn't worried about that in college. My goal was to get at least a 3.5 GPA and experience the very best time of my life (and that is exactly what I did). In the end, I would still have an engineering degree from Texas A&M University.

A&M is known for engineering, traditions, and football, so I dove deep into all 3, starting by embracing a four-and-a-half-year graduation plan that would allow me to enjoy a fifth football season on campus. Although I went to class every day in the Zachry Engineering building and became friends with some of my fellow engineers, I spent every moment of free time on the other side of campus in the student center. I entrenched myself in joining and serving in all things related to student government and leadership positions - - Fish Camp, Traditions Council, Muster Committee, Town Hall, and Hospitality. These organizations led to all my favorite college memories and taught me about collaboration, integrity, and having fun through serving others. And I eventually shifted to Industrial Engineering (IE), which was much more aligned with what I enjoyed. To me, I saw industrial engineering as having two paths - one more blue-collar on the manufacturing side and one more white-collar on the consulting or operations side. Both paths aligned to my core strength, which was driving efficiency out of any situation.

CHAPTER 6

One Phone Call Can Change an Entire Career.

When I started looking for my first professional job in 1999, the market was red hot due to the brewing tech boom. Every Big Five consulting firm was on campus looking for technology and business interns and full-time employees, along with every oil and gas company and big tech organization. Enron and Andersen Consulting recruited heavily as well, years before the scandal that put both companies out of business. I think I still have my Enron T-shirt. These companies were "wining and dining" the students, offering huge signing bonuses and dangling an extremely tempting "work hard, play hard" culture. One of my favorite recruiting experiences was with Price Waterhouse Coopers (PWC), who hired consultants. They flew at least a hundred of us to Colorado, fed us extravagant foods, put us up in gorgeous accommodations, and took us whitewater rafting down the Royal Gorge. At the end of the weekend, they handed us an offer letter with a large salary and a signing bonus.

The market was hot! The tech boom was exploding, and the dot com bubble hadn't burst yet, so graduates were choosing between the predictable life of big corporations and the risky path of tech start-ups in Silicon Valley. Given the very expected and well-planned life I was following, of course, I only considered the large, established organizations. The thought that I had nothing to lose at 22 years old and could chase any interesting opportunity wherever it led me never crossed my mind. In hindsight, do I wish I had moved to Europe, joined a startup, and moonlighted as a bartender while I traveled around and discovered myself? Sure, but that thought never occurred to me then, and even if it had, the sheer instability of it would have been petrifying to me. I was doing exactly what I set out to do at the right time and in the right sequence. I believed that I could do it all, and I was determined to figure out how to do that.

So, I continued attending company presentations and exploring opportunities that came to campus just in case something special came through. That is when I learned about Sabre, the Dallas-based technology company owned by American Airlines that powers airline reservations. Sabre was looking for product development interns to work on their Airline Solutions team. I honestly didn't want to be a product developer, but those are the types of corporate jobs available to an Industrial Engineer. The best part was I could fly practically free to anywhere that American Airlines traveled.

After reading about Sabre at the Career Center and signing up for an interview, I went to the company presentation. The speaker's name was Brett, and he was the Vice President of Product Development. He gave an interesting presentation about Sabre and the products, coding, and technical roadmap that we would be working on if we secured internships. When he opened the room for questions, I raised my hand. Brett called on me, and I said, "Will I ever get to work with people, or will I be behind a computer all day?"

In hindsight, this question was pretty naive and obviously uninformed about corporate life, but I do believe it set me apart from the male-dominated, fairly introverted engineers in the room. Brett laughed, along with the whole room, and then he said, "Yes, of course, you will work with product managers and other interns." He went on to explain the intern community and the socials we would be having all summer long with a little more about the culture of Sabre. I learned right then that the job, any job, is so much more than the daily functions and responsibilities. Ambitious career-minded job seekers choose companies based on the people who work there.

The next morning, I walked into my Product Development intern interview, and Brett was sitting on the other side of the table. He greeted me and said, "Oh, it's my little people person." He remembered me from the night before, and it immediately broke the ice. I learned to always ask a relevant question in a session like that if I want the speaker to remember me for a certain quality. In this case, I wanted Brett to know that I was well-rounded, not two-dimensional, and I cared about a career, not just a job.

I ended up getting the internship at Sabre for the summer of 1999, but the night before my internship, I received a phone call from Brett. This one call changed the entire course of my career. He said, "We had a reorganization at Sabre today. I am no longer the Vice President of Product Development. I am now the Vice President of Product Marketing. How would you like to come with me and do marketing for the summer?" He went on to share that my question at the session and our follow-up discussion the next day in my interview gave him the idea that I would enjoy marketing and working more closely with people.

I immediately said, "Yes, absolutely!" I have been doing marketing ever since. On that day, I trusted that Brett wouldn't lead me astray or put me in a position to be unsuccessful. Brett didn't know me, but his belief in my potential and his view of me as a full person, rather than just an engineering degree, enabled me to pursue an entirely different career direction. I wanted that engineering degree because I believe in making the most of the opportunities we have been given, but I had to trust that doors open for a reason. This was a God moment. God had a plan when he put Brett in my life.

Sometimes, life-changing opportunities come to us in unexpected ways. I had to yield my own tendency to plan and pursue achievement to hear God as He opened the door to new adventures.

On December 18, 1999, after a successful summer internship at Sabre and a final football season at Texas A&M, I graduated Cum Laude with a Bachelor of Science in Industrial Engineering and began my full-time career in product marketing at Sabre the following week.

PART 3

Reflections from Sabbatical

In 2021, 23 years into my career, I found myself at a crossroads entering this new chapter of my sabbatical. In the spirit of being an achiever, I had to learn how to take six months of extended time off from the daily grind. Waking up without an agenda and resisting the urge to check my email every five minutes was unnatural for me and forced me to lean into the open space. In the beginning, I felt the need to fill every second with something, almost like I needed to assure my husband (or myself) every evening that I had, in fact, accomplished something that day, even if I was not working right now. My husband Jim would say, "You know you don't have to do something every day. You can just relax, sleep, watch TV, and enjoy the downtime." That was counter to every part of my wiring, but it was exactly what I needed to do to truly give my mind and body time to rest. As I got a taste of precious Kelly time, I wanted more of it. I loved my quiet moments of reflection that weren't clouded by a never-ending to-do list and action items. I could just be.

As I reflected on my career and the lessons I learned along the way, I started to appreciate the themes that emerged that weren't entirely obvious in the moment but were crystal clear in hindsight. Some of the stories are funny now but were often painful in the moment, yet they have all served to make me a better leader, wife, mother, daughter, and friend with more empathy and compassion. Some of my leaders have been excellent, while others were terrible; some have been narcissists who are more worried about their image than their impact. I have worked for incredibly capable, brilliant, effective managers who are highly unlikable with deep character flaws. I have watched some of the nicest, most altruistic leaders bring their kindness to the office only to be trampled by greedy, power-hungry backstabbers who chopped their knees out from under them to get ahead.

Each of these stories has impacted my leadership at home and at work, both in what I want to emulate and what I hope never to be. They have all delivered lessons that have opened my eyes and inspired hope for the future. According to DesiringGod.org, "Hope" is the confident expectation of and longing for the promised blessings of righteousness. Biblical hope not only desires something good for the future—it expects it to happen. Every story, good or bad, reminds me that God is in control and He has a purpose in everything.

These are some of my stories.

Believe In Yourself First.
Others Will Follow.

As an engineer turned marketer, I had the opportunity to round out my skill sets as more of a business athlete. I had been considering business school for a few years since starting my career, given that I was essentially making up marketing as I went along. I never took a business class in college, but now that I was operating in a marketing capacity, I wanted to better understand the science, not just the art, behind marketing. The longing to want to apply to business school surprised me, given that it wasn't a step that I had pre-defined in my plan, but a multi-disciplined project in Brazil with Sabre helped confirm my decision. I was ready to explore learning beyond engineering and pivot my career toward business and leadership.

I had already taken the GMAT, which was required for the application at every school, but I wasn't happy with my score. I have learned throughout my life that there are many different flavors of "smart." There were the kids who studied hard to get good grades, and there were the ones who were creative and often tested as Gifted and Talented. Then there were those who were just naturally intelligent enough, and one quick skim of the material ensured an A most of the time. That last one was where I landed. I didn't study much, and I was never a GT kid. For me, most of my brain power came from an intense understanding of math and how numbers worked together, combined with a really good memory. The challenge with standardized tests, at least based on my experience, was that it wasn't all math or memory. It was a mix of thinking on my feet, using logic, and deducing conclusions from the material presented. I tended to do "fine," but never excellent.

Nothing about my GMAT scores screamed Ivy League, but as a perpetual believer in myself and that anything is possible, I swung for the moon. A dear friend, Alex, a fellow Christ follower who was a year ahead of me at Texas A&M and was now a first-year student at Harvard Business School, encouraged me to go for it and helped coach me through the process. I remember the HBS application vividly. There were six specific essay questions, each with a word count limit, and there was one extra opportunity for me to provide any additional insight that I wanted HBS Admissions to know about me. Alex shared with me that he felt that HBS was looking for the most well-rounded leaders, gifted with both IQ and EQ, not necessarily the highest-scoring, IQ-only intellects. I leaned into that.

I chose six different stories that I thought were meaningful to share, representing the broadest picture of who I was as an individual—everything from my beliefs to ethical dilemmas to opportunities to step up as a leader. For the bonus essay, I chose to explain how I felt that my GMAT score was irrelevant to the leader I would become. I shared the perspective that I felt that I could bring to HBS based on my extensive leadership experience at Texas A&M, my deep technical understanding of science, math, and engineering, and my passion for making a positive impact in the world. I told the HBS Admissions team that I believed that their number one priority was to be proud of the HBS graduates 20, 30, or 40 years later, knowing that the Harvard brand is associated with the integrity, compassion, and achievement of well-rounded leaders who are changing the world. Jeffrey Skilling, the infamous CEO of Enron during the very public scandal, was an HBS alum who was frequently in the news around this time, providing a negative impression of the quality and integrity of leaders coming out of Harvard. I represented the other side. Obviously, I could do the work. I graduated with honors in Engineering from Texas A&M. I just needed them to believe that I was more than a GPA or a GMAT score. I read, re-read, and edited those essays until they were perfect. And then I hit submit and waited.

Over the next few months, I learned that I had been accepted to McCombs at UT and Anderson at UCLA. I was declined admission to Columbia. Finally, I received an email from HBS that said:

"Dear Kelly:

Warm greetings from Harvard Business School!

After careful consideration of your application materials, we would like to get to know you better. This is our invitation to interview.

Take a moment and exhale. Then keep reading."

I was ecstatic. I learned that about 1,800 of the 10,000 applicants every year receive invitations to interview, and then about 60% of those are admitted. I believed that if I could just get in front of them, face-to-face, then I would have the opportunity to win them over. This was the moment that I needed.

Interviews were conducted by HBS alumni all over the world, but there were no alumni near me. Since I had flight benefits, I offered to fly myself up to Boston to meet in person, thinking that this showed initiative and my passion for HBS. On Monday, February 24, 2003, I headed to DFW en route to Boston. That day, a massive winter storm hit Dallas and left 3" of ice, sleet, and snow on the runways. DFW shut down. I would not make it to Boston that night nor arrive in time for my Harvard interview the next morning. After some pitiful tears, I notified my interviewer that I was stuck at DFW Airport and that I would need to conduct the interview over the phone. I walked to every terminal at DFW until I found the perfect quiet spot to speak to the HBS alum. I tried to remain focused and articulate from a corner of the airport after a night of sleep on a cot and a "shower" in the bathroom sink. I worked hard to remind myself that day that God has a plan that does not always align with mine, but His plan is perfect. I had to trust that these things work out exactly as they are supposed to. With that in mind, I was able to settle into the situation, muster up all the preparation that I had done, and pray for the best. The interview ended up going well, even if it wasn't at all what I expected.

On HBS notification day, I was in Sao Paulo, Brazil. We were on a dial-up network with only one cable in the conference room. My boss's boss was in town with me for the week, and she had priority over the network cable. At one point, I borrowed the cord, logged into my HBS account, and saw the notice for their admissions decision. A letter from the HBS Admissions Office read:

"Dear Kelly:

Congratulations and welcome! On behalf of the entire Admissions Board, it is with great pleasure that I invite you to join the Harvard Business School Class of 2005."

I had been accepted into Harvard Business School.

I was in shock, frantically trying to digest what I just read while trying to get through a meeting so that I could call my family and give them the news. I had never felt so far away from them. My boss's boss was pulling the network cable from my laptop, and I was trying my best not to let my excitement show as I was not quite sure what to tell my company about my decision to apply to a 2-year graduate program that would require me to leave my job. I will never forget that moment of exhilaration, panic, loneliness, nervousness, and pride that all came over me at the same time. How did this small-town girl from Texas end up in Brazil, finding out that she was accepted to Harvard in Boston, Mass? The Lord had certainly orchestrated the whole thing, but I also know that by believing in myself first, I was able to display the confidence and competence for HBS to believe in me too. I knew that I was capable and would add tremendous value to the HBS family. I just needed them to see it.

Over the next few months, I prepared for the move to Cambridge, Massachusetts. I was unprepared for the sticker shock of housing. I was also extremely nervous about moving to a new city in the Northeast with a very different culture, climate, and community from what I knew. Once I settled in, I fully immersed myself in the life of a Harvard Business School student. Stephen Covey, author of *The 7 Habits of Highly Effective People*, stopped by on the first day to welcome our class to HBS. After that, I spent a lot of time on campus, getting to know my classmates. I dug deep into the case studies to learn as much as I could about other industries and companies. HBS is a 100% case study method, so I would put myself in the protagonists' shoes three times a day, every day.

Over the next two years, I would get a chance to learn about Fortune 500 companies and how they solved their business challenges. And often, the protagonists themselves would come to campus to tell their story and share what happened. I remember such famous faces as Oprah Winfrey, Mark Cuban, and Warren Buffett. I was in a constant state of awe, humbled by the fact that I was standing in the halls of the most prestigious university in the world, that I was hearing from the leaders themselves about their companies that literally changed the economic landscape, and that I was surrounded by students from over 60 countries who worked in such places as the White House, the National Football League, the battlefields of Afghanistan, a micro-finance company in Rwanda, or on a major movie set in Hollywood. The stories around me blew my mind, often causing me to question how I got there.

We were divided into ten sections of 90 students each and spent the entire first year in one room with our section mates, changing seats only once during the semester break. I spent one semester on the first row, affectionately known as the worm deck, and one on the back row in the sky deck. Professors rotated through, but we stayed put, allowing us to develop deep, personal relationships with the people around us and find a place to call home in this larger-than-life program. Our section chair was Gail McGovern, former Executive Vice President of AT&T and President of Fidelity, who had previously been named one of the Top 50 Most Powerful Women in Corporate America in 2000 and 2001. She was a Columbia MBA, and she chose to give back by teaching marketing to future business leaders at HBS. On the first day of class, I remember her telling us that "our future bridesmaids and groomsmen are in this room." The thought of getting to that point of intimacy with these strangers seemed like a foreign concept to me. We were all so very different, and yet, over the next two years, I found my people.

Some of that bonding happened when, one day, a group of 10 of us decided to drive out to Concord to play golf. I ended up being the only female that played. We caravanned both ways, but on the way home, one of my friends and section-mates in another car was pulled over by a policeman. We all stopped and waited to make sure everything was okay as he stepped out of his old station wagon with flames painted down the sides. I don't remember what he did wrong, but the end result was that he was not allowed to drive home. He asked us, "Can anyone drive a stick shift?" I waited, assuming that one of these nine Harvard-educated men could drive a manual transmission. No one answered, and it turned out that half of them didn't even have a driver's license. Finally, I said, "I can drive a stick." The men around me were floored. I drove that beast of a vehicle home, orange flames and all, and I realized at that moment why a small-town girl from Texas was at HBS. It's because we can drive a stick.

And yet, my ability to drive a standard transmission wasn't the only area in which I found myself to be a minority. I learned very quickly that conversations about religion at HBS were very different from conversations in South Texas. Back home, the big question was, "What church do you go to?" But in Cambridge, I found myself in a land of "Wow, you're a Christian? I didn't know if there were any here." But, although I was a minority in my beliefs, I was not alone. I became involved in—and eventually the president of—the Harvard Christian Fellowship (HCF). This was a small community of HBS believers who were in constant fellowship and prayer for our classmates, for the university, and for the world.

The beautiful thing about being a Jesus follower in a foreign land is that I had a real opportunity to share my faith with folks who had never heard the Gospel. Despite living in an environment of incredible success and self-driven achievements, Harvard students aren't always seeking hope in something bigger. The majority often attribute success to their own individual achievements, so breaking through was not always easy. However, despite the extreme diversity among the students, I experienced more tolerance, understanding, and respect than I have ever experienced in the Bible Belt. I was exposed every single day to new cultures, religions, and ways of life, and after growing up in a fairly homogeneous town where most folks were at least nominal Christians with a conservative outlook, I learned to appreciate and respect differences, whether I agreed with them or not. This was a place where I had the opportunity to love unconditionally, learn about other beliefs and lifestyles, and test my own faith and fortitude. In John 13:34, Jesus says to *"Love one another. As I have loved you, so you must love one another."* I loved my HBS community fiercely.

Along with hard work and deep conversations about differing perspectives, life at HBS also involved lots of fun. We went skiing in Stowe, Vermont, and spent one Spring Break in Costa Rica with more than 200 of our classmates and the other Spring Break acting like teenagers on a Caribbean cruise. We hosted section socials at the Hong Kong in Harvard Square, and I met with four good friends every morning as a study group before class to review the cases. We watched the entire series of *24*, each season aligned to the clock over a 24-hour period. I also shared the entire box set of

The OC with my friends back when DVDs were the main source of movie watching. By the time I graduated, the DVDs didn't even work because they had been circulated through the hands of hundreds of my classmates.

I went on career treks to Chicago, NYC, Minneapolis, Los Angeles, and San Francisco. The flight might have been the most memorable part of that San Francisco trip, as I sat in first class with Sean Penn. He was flying home from Iraq, where he had just gone to write an article for the *San Francisco Chronicle*, and he'd had a layover in Boston. I acted like I had no idea who he was and tried to piece together a meaningful conversation despite my tongue being tied and my heart racing. I mentioned to him that I was flying in from Boston, and he said that he just finished doing some work out there. Obviously, as the perpetual *People* magazine reader, I knew this was the movie *Mystic River,* but I just nodded. I like to think that he appreciated a few hours of anonymity, even if I went to the bathroom, grabbed a flight attendant, and whisper-screamed, "Is that Sean Penn???" Needless to say, during my entire time at HBS, I was experiencing the opportunity of a lifetime, and I felt extremely blessed.

Believe in yourself and pursue the dreams that feel unreachable. Trust that God is in charge, but put in the work and advocate for the value you can bring. My friend Cathy used to say, "Even if it's God's will for you to win the lottery, you still have to buy a ticket." Aspire for greatness, and *Go For It*! No one knows what you are capable of more than you.

Story 1 Takeaways:

- **Aspire for greatness.** Dream big and take action towards making it a reality. Pursue what may seem unreachable.

- **Advocate for yourself.** No one cares more about your journey than you do. Have confidence in your abilities. Don't let limitations define your potential. Own your story.

- **Always be learning.** Broaden your skill sets and explore new fields, even if they weren't part of the original plan.

- **Trust the journey.** Know that it is part of something bigger that is beyond your imagination.

- **Embrace and appreciate differences.** Regardless of people, beliefs, and lifestyles, engage in conversations that challenge your perspectives and allow you to grow.

STORY 2

Stay Open to It.

Sometimes, the greatest opportunities come along simply because we are available. We just have to say, "Yes!"

One night in 2005, when I was living in NYC, I came home from work with plans to meet my friend Sophia for dinner. She had to cancel for some reason, but before I settled in for the night at home, my friend Jim called. I met Jim as an MBA summer intern at Kraft Foods the summer before. He had been doing his internship between his two years of business school at Kellogg School of Management at Northwestern. There were eight or ten of us interns from across various MBA programs like Harvard, Kellogg, University of North Carolina, Duke, Michigan, and NYU. During our summer internship hangout nights, Jim and I immediately discovered a shared passion for *The OC* and Baileys on ice. At the end of the summer, all the interns went their separate ways to finish the 2nd year of graduate school. I went to Boston, and Jim went to Evanston, IL, and the whole group stayed in touch loosely throughout the year. Jim knew from our group emails that I returned to Kraft, but he had not. He did move to NYC, however, but he lived in the outer borough of Staten Island and began a career in commercial real estate.

On the night Jim called, he said that he was on the Upper West Side and wanted to know if I wanted to grab a drink at a bar called Bourbon Street, which was two blocks from my apartment. I normally might have been lazy, but since Sophia had just postponed our plans as well, I was still dressed to go out. So, I agreed to meet him.

When I arrived at Bourbon Street, it was as if no time had passed. Jim and I had a couple of beers and laughed a lot. After a couple of hours, we walked outside to say our goodbyes. I leaned in for a quick hug, but he held on just a few seconds too long. It was at that moment that I realized Jim might have a little crush on me—and that was awkward.

A couple of days later, Jim called to let me know that he was going to be back in the city that weekend and wanted to see if I wanted to grab brunch somewhere. I didn't know whether this was a date or just another hangout, but it soon became clear that his intentions were plutonic when he showed up in a faded Syracuse sweatshirt, and I learned that "brunch" meant a sports bar. I found out later that this was on purpose, so that he didn't seem too eager. As usual, we had a blast and laughed the whole time, but Jim was firmly friend-zoned in my mind.

After brunch, Jim walked me back to my apartment. When we arrived at the front steps of my brownstone, Jim quickly said, "What do you think about being more than friends?" *What?* My mind went to a thousand different places in the three seconds it took me to respond. I was thinking, *No way! Can't we just be friends? Don't make this awkward. I have no interest in a relationship.* In that moment, however, I was more impressed by his confidence and directness than inconvenienced by his desire to ruin a perfectly good friendship with romance. No games. No minced words. No awkward, "Are we, or aren't we?" I just kept thinking, *Wow, that took a lot of balls to just come right out and say that.* So, I shrugged and said, "I'm open to it...I guess."

Despite my less than enthusiastic response, he grinned and said, "Okay! That is a lot better than what I was expecting." I think he said something about calling me later and then ran off quickly before I had a chance to change my mind. I found out later that what he was really thinking was, *So you're saying there's a chance.*

I also discovered over time that Jim had had a crush on me the previous summer during our internship, but he had kept that little insight to himself. He did, however, tell his best friend, Andy. So, that first night after leaving Bourbon Street and after the seemingly endless hug, Jim got in his car and immediately called Andy. Based on my understanding from Jim, his conversation went something like this:

Jim: "Hey, remember that girl from last summer that I had a crush on?"

Andy: "Yep, the one that wasn't available?"

Jim: "Yep. That's the one. Guess what? She's single now!"

Andy: "Dude, go for it."

Jim: "But we're friends."

Andy: "So what? You've got enough friends. If she says no, who cares? Will your life be any different?"

Leading up to our first "official" date, I was excited to go out but believed firmly that this was a one-date reward for his confidence and candor in asking me out. From there, I hoped we would table this romance thing, and a reignited friendship would ensue. That next Friday night, Jim and I went to a Knicks game at Madison Square Garden. Is there any better place for a first date? He bought me a hot dog and a beer, and I never watched a single play of the game. We talked and laughed throughout the entire game, and I realized that this man was brilliant, funny, and incredibly kind. We loved the same things and just "got" each other in the way that we saw the world around politics, personal responsibility, family, and faith. At the end of the evening, he hugged me good night, and I went home, surprisingly hoping for a second date. Something had clicked that night, and I began to develop a little crush on Jim.

Jim and I ended up dating for nine months, were engaged for nine months, got married, got pregnant on day 12 of the honeymoon, now have three beautiful children, and are going on 17 years of marriage. We live a joyful, fulfilling life together—all because I said yes to Jim on that first date. Being open to it forced me to take my controlling hand off of the steering wheel and trust that God had a plan. I may not have been particularly interested in Jim in that way at the beginning, but the Lord knew better and dropped Jim into my life at exactly the right moment.

And God didn't stop with Jim either. He has orchestrated every moment in my professional life as well. Before I began my summer internship in college, my boss Brett at Sabre asked if I would consider doing product marketing for the summer instead of product development as I had been trained. I said, "Yes, I'm open to it." I spent the rest of my career in marketing. Then when Sabre needed someone to scope a project in Sao Paulo, I volunteered because I was ready and willing (and happened to have a Brazilian visa).

When I was managing cheese at Kraft in Chicago following the birth of my first son Vann, my friend Joni from college knew that I wanted to get back home to Texas.

She recommended me to her boss, Margaret, who then reached out and offered me a job at Dell in Austin.

Margaret later left Dell for AMD and recommended me to the Vice President of Brand, John, who hired me at AMD at seven months pregnant with my second son, Henry.

My work at AMD caught the attention of another leader, JT, the future Chief Marketing Officer, who expanded my role to include product marketing.

Lisa, the Chief Operating Officer and eventual Chief Executive Officer at AMD, heard about me from JT and saw the work I was doing, and reached out to invite me to be her chief of staff.

One of Lisa's direct reports, Saeid, the General Manager of the Semi-Custom Business Unit, saw the work I did for Lisa and asked me to lead business operations for his organization.

Dave, the VP of Communications whom I worked with at AMD, called me from Rackspace to offer me a job leading Brand.

Carla was then hired as CMO over Dave, and within a couple of months, she pulled me out from under Dave, promoted me, and expanded my scope.

David, our Chief Product Officer, met me in one of Carla's staff meetings and then reached out to ask me to move to his team to set up a solutions marketing function.

When Carla left Rackspace, she was unable to speak at the Texas Conference for Women and asked me to take her spot to discuss failure and resilience.

A couple of years later, she recommended me to the recruiter at Gartner for the CMO role.

Two years later, my former colleague from Rackspace recommended me for the CMO role at a technology staffing company.

Great leaders open doors for other high-potential up-and-coming leaders.

And despite the one disaster of my last experience, I am still batting close to 1,000 on career progression because I was open to following inspiring leaders wherever they took me. I have been so blessed that God kept my heart open to it, but I often wonder how I have had so many powerful allies working in my favor throughout my career. The only logical conclusion that makes sense to me is that God is sovereign. He had an ultimate purpose for my life, and the roles I have been in were the perfect position at the perfect moment in His perfect plan. I pray relentlessly for God's will to be done and for the sheer honor of getting to be a part of it somehow. My career path is one small way where I can hopefully bring glory to Him in the corporate world where the presence of God is so desperately needed. My job is my mission field.

It is so easy to settle into a routine or even a rut in our current roles because it is safe, stable, and predictable, but we are often called to so much more. Don't get me wrong. Finish what you start and maximize every learning from your existing opportunity. But keep your eyes and ears open. Follow the market and skate to where the puck is going. Take those coffees that former colleagues or strangers request because they may open doors that you didn't even know existed. Start with an open posture, even if it turns out to be nothing. Stay open to it. All we have to do is just say, "Yes."

Story 2 Takeaways:

- **Just say "Yes."** Be open to it. The possibilities are more than you can imagine.

- **Cultivate authentic relationships.** They could open doors to future opportunities.

- **Trust that the timing is always perfect.** Don't dismiss opportunities too quickly. Give them a chance to unfold and reveal their potential.

- **Appreciate direct communication.** A straightforward approach leaves little chance of misinterpretation.

- **Lean into change.** While stability has its merits, being open to new challenges and ideas can introduce growth opportunities that you could have never dreamed of on your own.

Consumer Packaged Goods is the Ultimate Marketing Training Ground.

Fresh out of business school, I started work at Kraft Foods in East Hanover, New Jersey. My former roommate Mandie, from our previous summer internship, also returned to Kraft and was living in New York City, so we planned to commute to New Jersey together every day by car. Neither of us had a parking garage, so we were both at the mercy of street parking availability in the evenings. Between the competition for spots and the headache of moving both our cars every night for street cleaning, we came up with a brilliant idea to have our cars "live" at the Kraft office in New Jersey. Then, we would just drive one of those cars into the city every night after work and trade off the pain of finding parking. It worked beautifully—unless the one car in the city got snowed in, or we both needed our cars at night, or there was an event nearby and no street parking available. But hey, we were young, and the inconvenience seemed minor compared to our delight in our own strategic ingenuity.

In my first two years at Kraft, I had the pleasure of getting to work on Chips Ahoy! and Nutter Butter cookies, two of my favorites. Both were delicious for taste tests but not so accommodating for my waistline. Chips Ahoy! had a generous marketing budget, so we were able to conduct extensive research, hire top-tier creative and media agencies, and buy advertising in prime outlets like TV and print. Social media and digital marketing were not prevalent then, so advertising online was perceived to be a waste of money. I loved working with the agencies on the creative briefs, the concept reviews, and the video and photo shoots. One time, when my mom came to visit, I invited her to a cookie photo shoot in the city. We were both so excited to go to a real studio in New York City for a big-time photo shoot, but after eight painstakingly slow hours watching a food stylist arrange chocolate chips on a beautiful honey-colored cookie and then slightly melting the chocolate with a mini propane blowtorch, we discovered that food photo shoots are not quite that riveting after all.

Chips Ahoy! was such a huge business that we tracked its performance daily. I carried around a cheat sheet that I updated every day with revenue, volume, price, package velocity, average facings per store, inventory, and deals happening per store (like 2/$5.00 at Walmart). I knew that when Walmart was running a deal, the velocity at supermarkets would decline, indicating a trend that Walmart was "sourcing," pulling traffic and revenue from its competitors. I learned the more quantitative side of marketing, and I loved that use of data to defend, troubleshoot, track growth or secure investment with senior leadership. Data has and will always be king when it comes to marketing contribution and acceleration (and our own job security, of course).

My favorite project that I worked on had already started by the time I joined the team, but I had the pleasure of driving it to completion. We conducted quantitative and qualitative research with our target market: moms aged 25 to 44 who buy cookies for their kids. We learned that brand matters, but chocolate chip cookies are often a commodity at the grocery store. They are in the bakery, there are multiple national brands, and there is always a store brand. This means that if one product falls short in any way, it's easy to replace in the shopping cart. And Chips Ahoy! fell short in a big way. Its packaging at that time was designed to be easy to open: a consumer would open the end, slide out the plastic cookie tray, and remove the cookies they wanted. But what the designers hadn't accounted for was how difficult it was to get the tray back into the packaging. The cookie eaters would either get frustrated and force the tray back in, usually ripping the packaging and eventually letting the cookies grow stale since there was no re-seal function, or dump the remaining cookies in a Ziploc bag and put them in the pantry unbranded. Neither option was ideal for brand recognition or loyalty. So, we worked with the packaging engineers and developed a patented technology for resealability. It included a lift tab and resealable cover that we branded as "Snack and Seal" and implemented it on the red bag, Chewy Chips Ahoy. We launched it with vast marketing fanfare and investment, and the technology then expanded across the Chips Ahoy, Oreo, and Fig Newton product lines. This resealable packaging was a huge success and is still in the market today. It has not only solved a customer challenge, but has also created differentiation across a fairly generic, commoditized category.

This was my first taste of great marketing. I learned that marketing is not just about branding or advertising, but rather about solving customer pain points and carving out a product positioning that differentiates a product in the market. We could have continued pumping media dollars into the market to build the brand, but our repeat purchases and brand loyalty would have remained stagnant or declined. Instead, we found the root of the problem by talking to real consumers and developed a robust, fully integrated, 360° plan to solve that challenge. This resulted in increased purchase frequency, which yielded higher product velocity, increased revenue, and permission to raise price based on brand loyalty. This project, along with the daily management of the velocity metrics, illustrated to me why consumer goods marketing is the best training ground for both marketers and general managers.

A few years later, I joined AMD as a Sr. Brand Manager and learned quickly that corporate branding in technology is very different than brand management in consumer-packaged goods. CPG brand managers run the business and own the P&L, making critical decisions about advertising spend, product roadmaps, and growth strategy. Brand managers in technology were much more isolated and defined as the folks who own the logo and usage guidelines. We were able to do a full brand redesign and create a new set of brand guidelines, but otherwise, corporate brand management felt limited in its ability to make an impact on the business. If you are serious about a marketing career, I would highly encourage anyone to do a stint in brand management at a consumer goods company. You will never approach marketing the same again. You will have a deeper, more insightful understanding of the business dynamics, the levers to pull when driving demand, and the equity associated with a household brand. There is no better marketing training ground in the world.

Story 3 Takeaways:

- **Be the CEO of your brand.** Consumer packaged goods allows you to understand all the levers to maximize revenue. Don't just be a marketer. Be a business athlete.

- **The power is in the numbers.** Use quantitative insights to understand market trends, defend strategies, troubleshoot issues, and secure investment from leadership.

- **Embrace a customer-first mindset.** Understand the pain points and needs of your target audience deeply and create solutions that resonate and differentiate in a crowded market.

- **There is more to marketing than advertising.** Implement comprehensive 360° plans that address consumer challenges, increase purchase frequency, boost revenue, and enhance brand loyalty. Think about packaging, pricing, presentation, and customer delight.

STORY 4

Live in NYC at least Once in Your Lifetime.

Life started over for me when I moved to New York City. It was a new beginning in a new place, and the city greeted me every morning with energy and creativity around every corner. Sarah Jessica Parker used to say that New York City was the fifth lady in *Sex and the City*. God created the opportunity to bring glory to His perfect plan by delivering me to this magical city with a fresh start and renewed hope right after I graduated from HBS.

I lived in a brownstone on the Upper West Side of Manhattan. And by "brownstone," I really mean a traditional New York apartment; it was made of stone, but inside, it's just a 4-story walk-up. The term "brownstone" always feels fancier than it is, at least at my price point, but I loved my 500-square-foot, 3rd-floor unit that cost me almost my entire month's salary just to cover the rent. I decided to live alone in this tiny 2-story, one-bedroom, 1-½ bath nook that was absolutely adorable at 82nd St. and Amsterdam Ave, near Cafe Lalo (from *You've Got Mail*) and Seinfeld's fictional residence from the show. There was a delicious brunch place on every corner, the Natural History Museum was a block away, and Central Park was just two blocks east. At any time of day or night, I could find any cuisine I wanted within a 5-minute walk—Ethiopian food, designer cupcakes, NY-style hotdogs, or high-end French cuisine. I walked everywhere, often hiking five miles or more on weekends up and down Manhattan. I shopped for high-end on Madison Ave and vintage on Columbus Ave. I once bought a pair of brand-new Stuart Weitzman animal fur stilettos in my perfect size for $25 (retail price: $250+) from a darling consignment boutique. I found a crazy evangelical church in Hell's Kitchen and my favorite restaurants in the Meatpacking District. I saw the real Frankie Valli sitting in the theater when I went to see Jersey Boys on Broadway. There is no place like New York.

It was only a few years after September 11, 2001, that I moved to New York, but it wouldn't be until 2006 that I truly felt the impact of that tragedy on the community. One night early that year, Jim and I went to see *The Chronicles of Narnia: The Lion, The Witch, and the Wardrobe* at the AMC movie theater on Broadway and W. 84th Street, just a couple blocks from my apartment. In the middle of the movie, two men in the audience raised their voices as they began a heated argument. I have no idea what they were fighting about, but I am not exaggerating when I say that the entire theater cleared out within 7 seconds of hearing that sound. No one grabbed their drink or popcorn, no one said a word—everyone just bolted for the doors as fast as possible. The people of NYC displayed very clearly that they had no risk tolerance anymore for any form of violence in a public place. My heart broke for what the city had been through. The events of 9/11 changed the city forever, implanting a small fear and hyper-awareness in every New Yorker about the risks right there inside of our little Manhattan bubble. I felt so much pride in the city. I felt blessed knowing that God led my path to this beautiful moment where, despite the size and namelessness that is often conveyed with New York City, I felt like a part of a community.

Once I settled into my life on the Upper West Side of New York, I mastered bodega shopping, learned to appreciate New York bagels, pizza, and hot dogs, and discovered my favorite cookies at LeVain Bakery (these giant double-chocolate, peanut butter delights that melt in the mouth). I bought produce and flowers from the corner markets, people-watched in Central Park, discovered hole-in-the-wall theaters to see off-Broadway shows (some good, some terrible) all over the city, and attended Christmas parties at fancy Upper East Side apartments with HBS friends. I also learned to live alone in a huge city that could be both crowded and lonely. There was an incredible freedom in coming home by myself and doing whatever I wanted without judgment or permission, but as an extrovert, I also needed people to process with out loud. I split my time evenly between nights out with friends and nights in by myself.

Independence in New York is different than living alone in small-town Texas. One night, I became a true New Yorker when I found a rat in my apartment. The beauty of a brownstone is that it is typically above or near restaurants or bodegas, so rats are prevalent. But this one was my fault. I stored some shelf-stable food in a box on the floor of my downstairs closet because I didn't have shelf space in the kitchen. I started hearing noises at night but just assumed they were the sounds of the bustling city outside. It turns out that a little family of rats got into that box of food. I screamed, jumped up on the coffee table, and called Jim. As a native Texan, I was more used to scorpions and snakes. Jim talked me through it, and then I scaled the furniture to grab my purse and sprinted for the door. I hustled around the corner to the hardware store where they sell these sticky pads that catch critters, and then I stashed them in corners all over the apartment. I was thankful to have my bedroom upstairs where the rats couldn't scale the spiral metal staircase. The next morning, I found my first rat wiggling around on the sticky pad while his feet were pinned in place.

Another night, I went with friends to the Meatpacking District to celebrate someone's birthday. (I remember seeing Chelsea Clinton that night at the same event. It's amazing how famous people are everywhere in New York City, but they can just blend into the background.) At the end of the night, which was about 2 a.m., I went outside to catch a taxi, but couldn't find one. This was long before Uber became a thing. After waving my hand fruitlessly for 15 minutes, I finally decided to take the subway home, but I fell asleep on the subway and woke up at the 125th Street stop in Harlem. I immediately jumped off the train to find homeless people and late-night folks sitting on the ground around me in every direction. I didn't panic (out loud), but I moved quickly toward the southbound train. Unfortunately, this was one of those stops where I had to exit the northbound train, go above ground, cross the street, and then take the stairs back down to catch the southbound train.

I realized at this moment that I was in a precarious position–a young girl, all by herself, in a neighborhood I didn't know, at 2:45 a.m. When I made it to the top of the stairs, I saw an available cab heading south and jumped in it. The crisis was averted until I figured out that I had no cash, so I asked the cab driver to take Broadway down so that I could stop at the Bank of America ATM. In hindsight, I recognize everything about this plan was not ideal. Fortunately, my cab driver was lovely, did not mind stopping, and delivered me safely to my apartment.

When I tell this story to friends, their eyes widen at how risky a situation this could have been. I agree, but I have always been extremely fortunate that by giving people the benefit of the doubt, they usually deliver. I start with trust until someone gives me a reason not to (rather than the reverse). Yes, I could have been mugged or hurt by folks at the subway station or in the cab, but I believe that the Lord is sovereign. He never puts us in a situation that we can't handle, and He calls us fervently to love and trust Him and to love and trust each other. The people of New York always proved to be kind to me.

Yes, the Lord was taking care of me, but that didn't mean I no longer needed my parents. I absolutely loved living in New York City, but it was also incredibly expensive. I remember one day, I called my dad from work. I was standing out in the parking lot, feeling a little pathetic and ashamed for having to make the call. Finally, I mustered up the courage to ask him if he could please deposit $100 into my bank account. I promised to pay him back, but I wasn't getting paid until two days later, and my electric bill wouldn't clear the next day unless I could borrow a few dollars. He knew how hard I was working, but he also knew how expensive New York City was, so without question, he deposited $1000 into my account within minutes. Yes, I wrote that correctly. He threw an extra zero on the end for good measure because that's what good dads do. They teach all the right things, including responsibility and trust, along the way, so when the time comes to ask for help, they just say "yes," with no questions asked. I was a Harvard MBA living in NYC with a professional career making good money by American standards, and I still needed help. I constantly asked myself, *How does the Starbucks barista survive in this town?* or *Where does the grocery store cashier commute from in order to afford her rent?*

Story 4 Takeaways:

- **Embrace a fresh start.** New cities mean new beginnings and opportunities. Approach changes with energy and hope.

- **Inspire creativity.** The vibrant atmosphere of New York City can infuse energy into your life and fuel your personal and professional growth.

- **Face your fears head on.** Overcome unexpected challenges in unfamiliar places with an open mind, a positive attitude, and resilience. Embrace uncertainty and discomfort as opportunities for growth.

- **Give people the benefit of the doubt.** Start with trust and kindness. People will often surprise you with a willingness to help in return.

- **Live within your means.** NYC is extremely expensive, regardless of your career or educational background. Grab five roommates, rent a 1-bedroom unit in the village, eat all of the delicious food, and spend days roaming the streets and experiencing life.

The Degree of Imposter Syndrome Depends on the Audience.

My entire life changed in four weeks in 2007. Jim and I moved to Chicago right before the wedding and then flew to Austin to get married. We went to Ladera in St. Lucia for our honeymoon, where I turned 30 on day six and got pregnant with our first child around day 12. We both wanted children, but we had no idea if it would take five days or five years. So, we winged it on the honeymoon, and we were ecstatic when it happened so quickly. We were due in mid-January 2008. New city, new marriage, a new decade, and now, a new baby.

We moved to Chicago because Jim was offered an opportunity to move with his company to their headquarters to do real estate development. Since Kraft was located in Chicago as well, we were blessed to be able to transfer together, where I began working in the Cheese and Dairy division. We bought a condo in Lincoln Square on the Brown Line, which split the difference between his office downtown in the Loop and mine in the suburb of Glenview. I was thrilled to own property again rather than waste money every month on rent, but it was 2007, so we would come to regret this decision within two years.

Early in June of that year, I had to go on a work trip to a dairy plant to learn about our cottage cheese production process. I was traveling with an operations manager, and I was only about eight weeks pregnant, so my team at work was not aware of my news yet. He noticed that I didn't drink any alcohol at dinner or coffee at breakfast and then confirmed his speculation that I was pregnant when I threw up at the dairy plant. Cottage cheese is disgusting, and the smell of it curdling was too much for my morning sickness. He kept the news quiet, but I realized that I was going to need to tell my team soon if I was going to continue doing cottage cheese tastings back at the office.

On January 9, 2008, Jim and I welcomed Vann Albert Hopping to the world via C-section, weighing in at 9 lbs 2 oz, 21 inches long, and perfectly healthy. Vann was my maiden name, and Albert was Jim's paternal grandfather's name. I immediately fell in love with this little human, even though I just met him. He looked just like Jim and was a happy, content little boy. Jim cut the cord and followed Vann to get cleaned up. I was wheeled into recovery, but the combination of the epidural, the anesthesia from the surgery, and the hormone rush of delivering a baby put my body into shock a bit during recovery. I was freezing, with my pulse racing, and covered in hot blankets, but my arms were too heavy to lift. They handed Vann to me as I tried to settle down and muster the strength to hold him. I couldn't wait to cradle this perfect little being, but my body just wasn't ready to cooperate. Eventually, the weight of the warm blankets stabilized me, and I was able to bond with my beautiful son.

After four days in the hospital, we loaded Vann's car seat into our Volkswagen Passat and headed home. I couldn't fathom that the doctors just let us leave the hospital with this baby in our car. Didn't they know that we had no idea what we were doing? I'm sure that the drive home consisted of Jim driving too fast (by my new mom, overly anxious standards at 15 mph) and me nervously turning around to check on Vann at every turn. Were we responsible enough to care for a child who would be 100% dependent on us for the next 18 years (at least)? According to WebMD.com, the term imposter syndrome describes someone who feels they aren't as capable as others think and fears that they'll be exposed as a fraud. That is exactly how we felt. We knew that God would not give us more than we could handle, and we were so ready for this baby, but at this point, we were imposters, following blindly and faking it until we made it.

Though we knew God believed in us, it took some time before we believed in ourselves. For example, I remember Vann's first bath through joyful tears, though the tears I shed at the time were anything but. I had all the fancy baby gadgets—baby tub, tiny monogrammed washcloths, baby shampoo, and soaps—but I was so nervous about how to hold on to a slippery little baby while washing him at the same time without it being a chaotic, traumatic experience for both of us. I placed Vann in a bouncy bath seat inside the real bathtub and started washing him. Somehow, over the next few minutes, I'm holding Vann sideways, trying to clean his whole body, and he is pooping all over my hand. I slip and fall down on the edge of the tub, and Jim finds me crying on the toilet, saying something along the lines of, "I'm going to be a terrible mother. I don't know what I'm doing."

Eventually, I learned that babies have very low expectations. They just want to be warm, fed, and safe. I didn't have to be an expert on day one because I had a lifetime to learn. My imposter syndrome about being a mom was much easier to manage than the professional kind because my audience weighed 10 pounds. The stakes were higher because this little life depended on me, but I had the freedom and flexibility to take my time to learn.

Unlike being a new mom, new leadership positions at work carry much larger visibility from the CEO, the board, our peers, and our teams. Once I reached the C-suite, I didn't feel that I had that same freedom of time and space to figure it all out. Within just a couple of weeks, I felt the need to establish my command by making critical decisions like who is on my team, what our key priorities are, how the organization is structured, and how the team will be measured.

I carried the heavy burden of the role, the function, and the company's expectations to assess quickly, make changes, and deliver a quick win. I remember getting advice from a mentor before I started my first CMO role at Gartner: "In your first three months, you should fire someone, hire someone, and promote someone." This would help garner the team's respect and demonstrate that I was not afraid to make tough decisions. At first, it felt to me more like a façade to distract from my imposter syndrome as a brand-new CMO. Fortunately, I learned that it gets easier after a few tries. Each CMO experience shortened the learning curve on the next one, so I was able to assess the talent quicker, restructure faster, establish goals immediately, and make the necessary changes in weeks rather than months.

I have also learned that walking in the door with the full confidence and unwavering support of the CEO and Board of Directors makes all the difference. Those interview conversations and pre-start date relationship-building moments with a future boss are critical to accelerating trust and empowerment on day one. Spend extended time with a new boss before ever stepping in the door. That focused time has allowed me to make an impact faster, walking in with confidence, believing in my own decision-making, quickly delivering a strategy, and establishing followership. Confidence inspires confidence, which yields bold decisions and a big impact. Finding a boss who believed in me from the beginning was the key to overcoming my own imposter syndrome. Maybe God used my husband and smiley baby to serve the same purpose in my role as a mom. They helped assure me every day that I was doing okay.

Story 5 Takeaways:

- **Capitalize on a shorter learning curve**. Each experience builds on the last, reducing the time it takes to assess, triangulate, and make an impact in future roles. Write down what you learn after each experience. You'll be shocked at how much you know.

- **Ask for help.** Stand on the shoulders of the leaders who came before you. Seek mentorship and wisdom from their experience to help inform your approach.

- **Build trust.** Invest time with your new boss and leadership team before you start. By establishing command of your function early, you will inspire their confidence and trust, so you can hit the ground running on day one.

- **Confidence begets confidence.** The more your team believes in you, the more you will trust yourself to make bold decisions without apology. Know your audience and level-set your expectations based on what they need from you.

- **Take time to grow in your role.** Whether it's personal or professional, leadership comes with visibility and high expectations, but you don't need to have all the answers immediately. Prioritize quality of impact over speed of execution.

STORY 6

God's Plan Is Always Perfect.

Soon after our first son was born in 2008, we realized that we wanted to get close to family. Raising a little boy in Chicago while Jim's parents remained in upstate New York and my parents stayed in Texas was not ideal. We decided to focus on getting to Austin, TX, where there were plenty of career opportunities and an hour's drive from my parents. Jim's opportunity came along first. He was currently working in real estate development, but this was 2008, and the real estate market was in a severe financial crisis. He was happy to get out of real estate, and as a Jesus follower and former military officer, Jim was feeling called to give back to the veteran community. He found a military and veteran staffing agency called Bradley Morris and met with one of the leaders, TJ, who turned out to be a fellow believer. Jim and TJ had an instant connection, and Jim landed a job as a recruiter for Bradley Morris. They agreed to hold his job for as long as it took for me to find a role in Austin as well.

I wanted to work in one of those sexy Austin start-ups. I was a part of these huge behemoth organizations like Sabre and Kraft Foods, and I was excited to try my hand at supporting the entrepreneurial world. I took for granted that my tier-one marketing experience at Kraft, plus my MBA from Harvard would open any door for me in Austin. However, on paper, I looked like someone who lived in Chicago and only worked for big, slow companies.

I flew down and met with multiple start-ups over a few months, and every one of them had the same concerns. Could I change my industry (from CPG to tech) and the size of the company (from big and slow with deep pockets to fast and scrappy with little to no resources) and still be successful?

One of the greatest lessons learned from business school came from the Director of the Career Center. He coached us on how to make a career pivot. Think of a pivot step in basketball—one foot stays planted, and the other rotates around. If we wanted to make a change, we needed to plant one foot somewhere we had experience first—a function, an industry, or a location— and then pivot the other two. Changing all three is often an impossible pill for a recruiter to swallow. For example, for a New York City investment banker to become a CPG brand marketer in Minneapolis would be a tough sell to recruiters as it requires a change of industry, function, and location. That's a lot of risk. However, staying in NYC and shifting to a corporate finance role at a CPG company would be an easier move to make. That candidate gets to plant her experience in finance in NYC while pivoting the industry to CPG. The next pivot, if the first one works out, could then be the move from finance over to brand marketing in CPG as originally desired. It may take two hops instead of one, but it builds on experience and sets her up for long-term success in the process.

In this pursuit of a move to Austin, I was trying to change *three* things, not one. I was trying to change industries, company size, *and* location, and it was too much to translate via a resume. So, I made the decision to switch industries first, shifting to tech, but staying in the big company space. We also began the process of finding somewhere to live in Austin. I believed that once I was a local Texan working in big tech, then I'd be able to move to any Austin start-up. That paid off over time.

I joined Dell based on a call from a Texas A&M industrial engineering friend, Joni, who worked in product planning on the Latitude commercial PC business. Her boss, Margaret, needed a product line manager and provided full relocation for our move from Chicago to Austin. The day I got offered the job, Jim was laid off from General Growth Properties (GGP) because of the real estate financial crisis. I saw God's hand all over it as we both now had jobs and relocation to Austin, but the exit from GGP would provide a nice severance for our already-planned move. It wasn't quite as rosy for Jim's pride, but he took it in stride and used it as an opportunity to spend a lot of one-on-one time with Vann for the next couple of weeks before the transition to Texas.

A few weeks later, we put our Chicago condo on the market in the middle of the declining real estate market. Our property value plummeted significantly below what we owed on the condo, so we would have to find a buyer in a massive down market and cover the gap between purchase price and mortgage payoff. Dell would buy the property as part of the relocation package, but the purchase price would be based on assessment value, not true market value, so we would owe a significant amount of money in that situation as well. I was overwhelmed by the stress. We both worked hard and had great educations and careers, yet we were about to write a check that would decimate our savings (and still not clear). I felt desperate about our situation and foolish for rushing to buy a place in a city where we weren't planning to stay long. I had it in my head from the beginning that rent was a waste of money.

We eventually found a buyer who offered well below asking, and we had to accept it, but I started doing research on how we could pull this off. I found out that the Obama administration was offering short-sell solutions for situations like ours. For context, a short sale is when a house is sold for less than the amount still owed on the mortgage, so the lender must approve that short sale and eat the costs. In this scenario, because of the nationwide real estate crisis, the Obama administration was forgiving short sale gaps and absorbing those costs from the lenders.

As hard-working Americans and Christians, Jim and I were both believers in putting in the work and not taking hand-outs from anyone, especially the government. 2 Thessalonians 3:7-8,10 says, *"For you yourselves know how you ought to imitate us, because we were not idle when we were with you, nor did we eat anyone's bread without paying for it, but with toil and labor we worked night and day, that we might not be a burden to any of you... If anyone is not willing to work, let him not eat."* We firmly believed that if we couldn't afford something, then we shouldn't buy it, never putting more on credit than we could afford. So, we struggled with this situation, not knowing quite how to view a short sell in 2009 in light of scripture. In the end, we decided to pursue the short sell. We were working hard and already bought the condo when we could afford it, but now we had to deal with that tremendous decrease in property value due to the macroeconomic conditions.

We submitted our request for a short sale and then prayed a lot. I called the short sell department every single day to ask for a status update on whether our account had been approved. Short-sell approvals could often take months or even a year to process and approve, especially if the government was involved. In the meantime, we were anxiously trying to line up help from wherever we could to figure out how to close on this property.

I should have been encouraged by Matthew 6:34, *"Therefore do not worry about tomorrow, for tomorrow will worry about itself. Each day has enough trouble of its own."* But I wasn't having that. I had been a nervous wreck about the possibility of massive debt, and once again, I learned the hard lesson about the side effects of stress on your body when I began losing clumps of hair from the side of my head. I was eventually diagnosed with Alopecia Areata (i.e., patchy baldness), and I could now add self-conscious and embarrassed to the list of growing adjectives for how I was feeling. I wore my hair up every single day to hide the ugliness. Fortunately, my Doogie Howser-like dermatologist, Dr. Boos, regenerated growth by injecting steroids around the 2.5" diameter bald spot, and eventually, my hair returned to its normal state.

I knew in my heart that I should have given all my anxiety up to the Lord, but sometimes, I just wanted to stew in my own stress. Praise God that He is sovereign regardless, and He proved it (yet again) just when we needed Him to. On the day before closing, when I made my daily call, I found out that we were finally approved for the short sale of our condo. Not only would we not have to write the big fat check, but our credit would not be affected at all. That is not usually the case, but this was a God moment. God's perfect timing allowed flexibility on the start date from Bradley Morris, an offer from Dell with relocation, a severance from GGP to help with moving and transition costs, and complete forgiveness on the lost value owed for our condo. The Lord's timing is always perfect, even if I forget that sometimes. Jeremiah 29:11 says, *"For I know the plans I have for you, declares the Lord, plans for welfare and not for evil, to give you a future and a hope."*

Story 6 Takeaways:

- **Leverage a career pivot strategy.** When changing careers or roles, leverage at least one existing experience as a foundation while making targeted pivots to new industries, functions, or locations. This approach can help mitigate risk and provide a smoother transition throughout your career.

- **Balance your values with practical decisions.** Evaluate situations based on both your beliefs and opportunity to ensure you are making the best life decision, not just a career choice.

- **Trust the timing and the process.** God's plan is always perfect. Even when things seem uncertain or stressful, understand that His plan is always the right one, even if it feels different from our own. We just can't see the full picture.

- **Listen to your body.** Stress and anxiety can affect you in a number of different ways. Recognize those physical and emotional effects and seek ways to manage the stress, whether through prayer, professional help, hobbies, or support from friends and family.

- **Have hope for the future.** Stay anchored in your faith and remain open to possibilities, even in uncertain times.

Traveling the World Expands Your Perspective.

During Christmas Break in my first year of business school, I went on a solo trip to Europe. I went through a bad breakup, and I needed time and space on my own. I flew to Madrid and then took trains to Barcelona, the French Riviera—Monaco, Nice, Cannes, and Saint-Tropez—and then on to Paris, and finally ended in London. I journaled every day, wandered the streets of each new city, visited beautiful museums, took siestas in the afternoon, watched *The Phantom of the Opera* in Spanish in Barcelona, stayed in hostels, took overnight trains from place to place to avoid lodging costs, and just tried to digest everything that had happened. One of my favorite memories of the trip happened in Barcelona. I found this beautiful restaurant on the beach, where you could get a three-course lunch and a half-carafe of wine for some ridiculously low price. I had a delicious meal of tapas and paella, and looking out over the water, I finished the wine with my dessert. Afterward, I walked back along the beach toward my hotel, but I was so tired that before I made it back to my lodgings, I secured my backpack under me and fell asleep on a bench for three hours. It was glorious and the most restful sleep I'd had in a long time.

Yet, despite all my incredible experiences, I learned quickly that I hated traveling alone. I absolutely loved Spain and France, but I am an extrovert, and I need to process out loud. As thoughts or revelations came into my head, I had no one to share them with. I would write them in my journal and send them in emails to my parents or close friends, but I needed the give-and-take of discussion with someone else. Still, I think God knew what he was doing in sending me on that trip alone. It forced me to dig deep into my own heart and not justify my perspective based on the opinions of others. I had to figure myself out first. Regardless, what a relief it was when I met one of my closest HBS friends, Sophia, in London for the last five days.

Following graduation from HBS, I took the summer off before starting work in September. My signing bonus from Kraft Foods, plus low-interest rates and easy accessibility to student loans throughout business school, allowed me the cash I needed to fund the summer before starting my post-MBA career. So, in June, I made a late decision to go on a two-month mission trip to Southeast Asia with a group from Intervarsity Christian Fellowship (ICF). I flew out a few weeks early to explore Australia and Thailand before the mission trip started. I spent a week in Sydney, where I fell in love with the Australian people, shopping, restaurants, and beaches.

I went from there to Thailand, where I toured Bangkok, Chiang Mai, Chiang Rai, Phuket, and Koh Samui for two weeks. I had the chance to visit the Karen Long Neck hill tribe in Chiang Mai, where the women wear brass coils up their necks, as well as the Akha hill tribe in Chiang Rai, where the women are adorned with colorful textiles and ornate headdresses covered with beads, silver buttons, and balls. I bought jewelry, fabric, and art from these impressive women. Then, I spent a couple of days relaxing on the beach in Koh Samui, where I experienced a two-hour Thai massage for $15. She rolled me in a ball and pounded out every negativity I had inside.

This was the summer of 2005, so when I arrived in Phuket, I was humbled by the aftermath of the 2004 tsunami, the deadliest one in recorded history. The city was trying to rebuild, but there was devastation where buildings, beaches, and homes were destroyed. I was in awe of the Phuket people who came together to bring the city back to its former glory.

Finally, I flew on to Singapore to begin non-profit work with ICF. I joined a small team of other recent MBA grads who also love Jesus, and we immediately gelled. We settled into student housing and explored Singapore every spare second we had. My favorite part was the Hawker centers, where we ate delicious foods like chili crab and barbecued stingray. Beyond eating, we shopped, visited the beautiful architecture, and completely disconnected from the world.

As part of our mission, we were working in partnership with Eagle Communications, a purpose-driven consulting firm that works with Asian leaders to help them live their lives to the fullest through their faith. They wanted to understand how these leaders incorporate their faith in the workplace differently based on their nationality and culture. Over four weeks, we traveled around Southeast Asia and interviewed CEOs from Singapore, Indonesia, Malaysia, and Thailand. I loved Jakarta, Indonesia. The people were friendly, the food was amazing, and the lifestyle was very different from what I was used to in the U.S.

Over time, our interviews drew very distinct conclusions. We learned that in Thailand, they didn't separate business from personal. A Thai CEO would pay someone out of his or her own pocket rather than fire them, while a Singaporean CEO was much more Western. Similar to the United States, a leader from Singapore would eliminate someone's job if underperforming or if he/she were no longer needed. It's just business. Malaysia and Indonesia fell somewhere in between. This data enabled Eagle Communications to better meet their clients where they were, understanding how their faith and nationality affected their business decisions.

Five years later, I returned to Asia on a business trip for the AMD brand launch. By this time, I had two sons—Vann was almost 3, and Henry was 7 months old. I was still nursing Henry and planned to for a year, just as I did with Vann. I squeezed my trip into as short of a timeline as possible to limit the amount of time I was gone. I left on a Sunday, flew to Beijing, arriving late Monday night, and then flew to Taiwan on Tuesday night, Singapore on Thursday morning, and then back to Austin on Friday night. I was gone five nights with extensive jet lag, but I wanted to keep my milk production on U.S. time, so I set alarms at all times of day and night to pump. I accumulated and carried bags of milk from one city to the next, storing the milk in hotel refrigerators along the way. By the time I neared the end of my trip, I had a full cooler of breast milk. However, at the Singapore airport, arguably the most western of the Asian cities, security would not let me through. The very intelligent female security agent said, "If that's breast milk, where's your baby?"

I took a deep breath, gritted my teeth, and said very directly, emphasizing each word, "If my baby was with me, the breast milk would be in him." Two hours later, and after multiple failed requests to keep the milk, the supervisor of security finally agreed to let me ship the milk under the plane with luggage. I had no choice as my plane was boarding, and it was winter, so I hoped that the cold temperature would possibly keep the milk from spoiling. I arrived in Austin to find out that the cooler of breast milk was lost. Three days later, the cooler showed up on my doorstep, full of spoiled, rotten, stinky milk, and I was forced to pour a week's worth of liquid gold down the drain. I was exhausted from the trip and furious about the wasted time and effort to pump and preserve that supply of milk for Henry. I carried so much guilt for going on that trip in the first place, leaving my husband alone for six days with two kids under 3 years old, that the feeling of letting Henry down with no milk to show for it was devastating for me. I'm sure jetlag exacerbated those feelings as well. In hindsight, I am grateful that I kept my production up while on the trip, even if that was all I came home with. I learned that the world was not entirely ready or equipped for working moms.

Regardless, traveling the world taught me to never take my own comforts for granted. It showed me how beautiful differences can be around the world in terms of how we think, how we live, what we eat, and how we conduct business. I was overcome with gratitude when I landed back on U.S. soil, but I was always itching to go back and see more.

Story 7 Takeaways:

- **Solo travel enables self-reflection.** Exploring new places by yourself in a foreign place is an incredible means of self-reflection and growth, allowing you to process your thoughts and feelings, learn more about yourself, and gain a deeper perspective and appreciation of your life.

- **Embrace cultural diversity.** Experiencing the diverse lifestyles of the world can help you develop open-mindedness and cultural sensitivity, which are critical in today's global business environment. Don't just travel from the airport to the hotel and back. Immerse yourself in the culture.

- **Recognize your privilege.** Every part of the world might not be ready for the privileges you have become accustomed to, which means every colleague you work with might be coming from a different perspective or expectation. Embrace the differences, be flexible and tolerant, and learn to adopt quick problem-solving skills to adapt to any situation.

- **Maintain a curious mindset.** Seek out new experiences anywhere you can. Always be learning. Always be exploring. Always be living.

- **Cherish the small joys of life.** Enjoy regional foods, admire unique art and architecture, and immerse yourself in local experiences. Appreciate the little things.

Lateral Moves Develop More Well-Rounded Leaders.

At the end of my two years at HBS, I never saw the world the same again. My business school experience transformed my perspective on human differences, economic opportunities, and the thousands of different ways that we can make an impact. I learned how to hone my leadership skills so that I could go back to the office and affect the lives around me. We spent more time focused on how experienced business executives conducted themselves as leaders, both good and bad, than we did on the technicalities of how to run a business. I was exposed to the world of exit strategies, learning how to choose between staying private, going public, or being acquired. I explored all the ways to fund and grow a new business between angel investors, raising venture capital funds, or sourcing other outside investment. I thought like a CEO, CFO, CMO, and COO, depending on the case, allowing me to get a taste of whichever career path seemed most interesting.

When I arrived at HBS, I knew I was planning to focus on marketing and, specifically, I wanted to shift to consumer marketing. I had just spent the last four years marketing to travel agencies, which were a dying breed thanks to the explosion of the dot com boom that yielded companies like Expedia, Travelocity, and Orbitz. I wanted to be a part of something relevant and growing. When companies started coming on campus in the spring of my first year to recruit summer interns, I focused on consumer-packaged goods (CPG). CPG was known to be the best training ground for marketers.

Remembering what I had learned from the Career Center, I knew that I wanted to keep one foot planted in marketing, but pivot industries to consumer packaged goods, and I didn't care about the location. Fortunately, as soon as I met the team from Kraft Foods, I quickly identified my number one choice. I loved the products—Nabisco cookies and crackers, Planters peanuts, Post cereals, DiGiorno pizza, and Kraft cheese—and the locations were ideal in New York and Chicago. I was able to craft an authentic narrative that made sense for my interviews. I was an engineer by trade but spent four years in tech marketing. I was now halfway through pursuing my MBA and wanted to learn hands-on practices from the very best in the brand marketing industry, and I wanted to be a consumer of my product so that I could market most effectively. I landed the internship and spent my summer working on specialty cookies like SnackWells, Peek Freans, and Lorna Doone at Kraft Foods. One key accomplishment that gives my mom and her friends something to be proud of was my project to redesign the Ginger Snaps box. Cookies were fun!

Five years later at AMD, after a successful brand relaunch, I discovered the limitations of the corporate brand in comparison to CPG brand management. I felt limited to logos and color palettes and serving as the brand police rather than contributing to growing a business. So, I began to aim higher at work. I started pitching leadership on ownership of the entire product brand portfolio, pushing to rationalize our logo set, redefine product positioning, and clarify our differentiation in the market. Leadership took notice and expanded my responsibility, eventually leading to a move to product marketing and our go-to-market campaign strategy for the commercial business. I led a small team for the first time under the VP of Product Marketing, JT, who turned out to be one of my favorite leaders of all time. He poured into me in a way that helped me realize how much I loved managing people, spotting key talent, developing their career paths, and providing strategic direction and objectives. Leadership gave me a sense of community and purpose, knowing that we were all in it together, aiming toward the same goal.

From corporate brand to product marketing to campaign strategy, all three roles were a lateral move. I had always thought that new roles and expanded responsibility usually meant promotions, but I came to appreciate the diversity of experience at the pre-director level, which is so critical to finding my professional gifts and discovering my passion. Once a leader achieves the director level in a certain function, it is often hard to avoid being typecast as "the brand person" or "the events person." Broadening my marketing experience prior to becoming an executive allowed me to show my depth and flexibility in leading multiple aspects of marketing, from brand to demand, and I had the chance to build and manage a team.

I always encourage young, up-and-coming marketers to take those lateral opportunities early to expand the types of director and VP opportunities later, even if it doesn't feel rewarded in the moment. Take advantage of every opportunity to broaden and diversify one's skill set and experiences early and often. Not only does it make you more marketable, it also enhances your perspective as a business athlete.

In addition, I don't believe that leadership experience can be short-sided. I have mid-level managers on my team who ask me all the time for a promotion. Yes, they may have absolutely mastered their functional craft, but learning to navigate internal bureaucracy, establish cross-functional influence, understand relationship dynamics, and read a room require time in seat. When I see those young, cocky managers come through at breakneck progression, my first thought is, *He/she hasn't been humbled yet.* Moving through the ranks quickly is proof of functional expertise and depth of hard skills, but leadership acumen and emotional intelligence in a professional setting require situational experience and time to observe, understand, and respond to effectively with much more complicated soft skills.

Story 8 Takeaways:

- **Leadership takes time.** Great leadership goes far beyond mastering technical or functional skills. Soft skills like developing emotional intelligence, navigating complex relationships, and mastering situational awareness require experience over time. Quick promotions do not always allow for a comprehensive understanding of leadership dynamics.

- **Gather experiences, not progressive job titles.** Recognize that lateral moves don't always result in immediate promotions, but the intangible benefits of a unique experience, broader skills, and a deeper understanding of the business will eventually pay off in more significant leadership opportunities.

- **Craft authentic narratives.** Learn to effectively communicate your story that highlights how each career step contributed to your unique value proposition. Focus on significant achievements or contributions that build credibility in progressing your career goals.

- **Diversify your responsibilities.** Embrace the idea that lateral moves offer a unique perspective that will yield more holistic learning and a much more versatile leadership style. The opportunity to expand your range is most prevalent at the pre-director level.

STORY 9

Find Meaning in the Suffering.

A few days after Henry's first birthday in 2011, we found out that I was pregnant again. Unlike my pregnancies with both Vann and Henry, when we intentionally left ourselves open to conceive, this time was different. We definitely wanted a third baby, but not yet. We had a 3-½-year-old and a 1-year-old who were both in daycare, and I was commuting for an hour each way every day to work at AMD. When we found out we were pregnant, we were pretty shaken up. I wasn't ready. I've always been wide open to God's plan for children, so I expected myself to be ecstatic at this incredible blessing. Instead, we were in shock and exhausted at the thought of parenting three kids well, much less continuing to work and paying for daycare for all of them. We were faithful and trusted God's sovereignty, but we were stunned by the news. Jim and I talked about it, prayed fervently, and thanked the Lord for His blessing, but also begged for the strength and energy to get ready and excited for this baby.

We went to the doctor two weeks later, and she confirmed that we were six weeks along. At that moment, God changed our hearts. He answered our prayers and lifted our worries, and we began to delight in the prospect of another baby. We started planning for the baby—picking baby names, figuring out the nursery, and envisioning how close our three kids would be as they grew up. At eight weeks, we went back to the doctor to hear the heartbeat for the first time, only that heartbeat never came. We miscarried.

Losing a child, even at such an early stage, is devastating as parents are forced to mourn the life of a baby they never had the chance to meet. We knew that God had a purpose for everything, but we were drained from this emotional rollercoaster. We spent two weeks trying to trust God in bringing us a baby that we weren't ready for, followed by two more weeks of renewed energy and spirit in anticipation of getting excited for that baby, only to have the bottom drop out again. I cried, and we prayed, reminding ourselves that God does not waste suffering and that He wants us to have a desperate daily dependence on Him so that we can both lean on Him and be a light for others through our own experiences. In 2 Corinthians 1:4, we learn that God the Father *"Comforts us in all our affliction so that we will be able to comfort those who are in any affliction with the comfort with which we ourselves are comforted by God."* That little tongue twister of scripture assures us that our pain provides perspective and comfort for others who go through similar heartache.

To be honest, I always felt like we were invincible after having two healthy babies, so the high achiever and recovering perfectionist in me struggled with feeling like I failed in my ability to carry this baby to term or that I did something wrong in the way I took care of our unborn baby. Maybe my feelings of doubt at the beginning somehow caused God to rethink His decision to bless us with another baby. Obviously, I completely underestimated the sheer magnitude of God and how much bigger He is than all of this, but every thought went through my head. As we grappled with feelings of failure and loss, we began to learn about miscarriages. We found out that about 10-15% of known pregnancies end in miscarriage. That is almost 1 in 7 pregnancies, so given that I already had two healthy babies, I came to terms with the fact that it wasn't my fault. God just had a different plan for that little one.

Within days of my miscarriage, my good friend and neighbor across the street also lost her pregnancy. My heart broke for her, and I fully realized

God's gift of empathy and compassion as I was able to support her in a way that wouldn't have been possible if I hadn't experienced the same pain. Once again, God showed me that He doesn't waste suffering.

Seven months later, when we were ready and fully healed from the miscarriage, we were finally ready to try for baby number three. At this point, we had two boys, so, as if we had any control at all, we decided to try for a baby girl. Obviously, a third boy would have been a gift as well, but we thought we might as well shoot for the stars. We prayed hard and scanned the internet for tips. Multiple people swore by the Chinese calendar, which predicted gender based on the day and month of conception. We looked back at the accuracy for Vann and Henry and discovered that they should both have been girls based on the Chinese calendar. Our theory was that the Chinese calendar didn't hold up since my boys were half-Korean. So, we aimed for a time when the calendar showed that we would have a boy, and lo and behold, we got a girl!

In late August 2012, Elsie James Hopping was born, weighing in at 8 lbs 5 oz, the smallest of my three kids. Elsie was the name of both mine and Jim's paternal grandmothers, so it was an easy choice for our little girl. (After Borden named their cow Elsie in 1936, the name dropped off in popularity as a girls' name, and we liked that, even 76 years later, it was still unique.) My husband's full name is James Kevin Hopping, Jr., but since we didn't have a JKH III, we decided to keep James in the family through her middle name. As a good southern gal, I made the case for calling her both names. To this day, my sweet girl still goes by Elsie James.

Our kids were all about 28 months apart, so we now had a newborn girl, a 2-⅓-year-old boy, and a 4-⅔-year-old boy, all living in a three-bedroom apartment while we built a new house. Elsie James slept in a Moses basket in the corner of the living room for her first four months. It was a full house, and it represented every joy we could ever imagine! That horrific pain of losing a baby to a miscarriage only made the delight of welcoming Elsie James that much sweeter. Praise Jesus that He has a purpose in everything, even when it's hard to understand in the process.

That same lesson has been clear in my career as well. I have somehow found myself in two decades of declining industries. I almost jokingly want to warn all my future bosses that if the business is thriving, the macro trends are about to change if they hire me. Short the stock! At Sabre, I worked on products for travel agents just as the dot com boom was surging and online retailers like Travelocity, Expedia, and Priceline were launching and putting mom-and-pop travel agents out of business. At Kraft, I marketed cookies just as the enemy shifted from fat to sugar and carbohydrates. At AMD, we saw the potential for where gaming processors could go, but our bread and butter was the consumer PC market, where Intel was dominating at 90+% market share, and AMD was struggling to deliver enough yield off their silicon production.

I joined Rackspace, which dominated the managed hosting space for the decade prior, just in time for Amazon and Google to cut public cloud costs in half, causing Rackspace to have to reposition itself. I led marketing for the small business division at Gartner when the COVID-19 pandemic hit in 2020 and put many small companies out of business. I was the CMO at HYCU, a VC-backed SaaS company, when Silicon Valley Bank, the banking and debt provider for most PE and VC companies, collapsed in 2023. And finally, when I was ready to publish this book, I signed a deal with Scribe Media on May 29th, and the very next day, on Tuesday, May 30th, news broke that Scribe was going out of business. If you want to know where the capital markets are going, follow my career and do the opposite.

Although my timing has been impeccably bad, I have learned the art of managing a business through a decline, which is often about minimizing costs while trying desperately to accelerate revenue. One of the largest cost drivers is headcount, so I have experienced my fair share of making the hard decision to lay off a portion of the workforce—assessing the individuals, restructuring the team for efficiency, and eliminating positions along the way. For me, the easy part is finding opportunities to operate thinner by reducing some of the priorities. This will naturally lead to a more streamlined workflow at a lower cost, but deciding who will lose their jobs makes the process much more difficult. If I am completely honest with myself, then I can usually identify a couple of lower performers where I know this is in the best interest of both parties. It's the gray area in between where the struggle is real. I often have competent individuals who do solid work but are just no longer needed based on the business environment.

During my time as VP at Rackspace, the company was taken private by Apollo Global Management, and our entire leadership team turned over. After a few months of lucrative uncertainty, as Apollo bought out all our shares at a premium, I had the opportunity to settle into my first experience working for a private company. Every company I had ever worked for in my professional career was publicly traded, which often prioritized short-sided quarterly earnings cycles over long-term customer acquisition and growth. Becoming a private company brought freedom to be able to think through strategic decisions and the right investment mix to affect the company's valuation over the next few years. This would ultimately help my development in my path to startup.

However, I also learned that most private equity firms are looking for a highly profitable turnaround and four-year exit, driven by customer growth, increased operating efficiencies, and sucking the soul out of the culture through spending cuts. The victim of privatization is the rapid decline of employee engagement as the company races to higher valuations and tries to accelerate exit timelines. As part of that optimization, I consolidated all the solutions, verticals, and product marketing teams under me and then was forced to lay off half of them.

Once I decided who would be affected, then the key was speed. Word gets out, people talk, and productivity screeches to a halt as everyone waits to see what happens and who will lose their jobs. Keeping the date confidential never seems to work, and the water cooler chat explodes into speculation and anxiety. The senior executives know what is happening and are trying to be as professional and thoughtful as possible to protect the employees, while individual contributors are starting to look for other jobs and secretly comparing themselves against their peer group to assess their risk potential.

During the exit conversations, I tried to remain loving yet stoic as I communicated the details of their severance packages. As a leader who has laid off dozens of team members, I have witnessed every possible reaction from the impacted parties. Some folks have been shocked, having obviously lived under a rock for the weeks prior, while others have come to the exit meeting with full transition plans, links to share drives, and heartfelt thank yous for the opportunity to have worked there. I have been screamed at and called every bad name in the book, only to receive an apology voicemail months later after reflection. One lady said, "Yes! We can finally be friends on Facebook." But I have also had my character questioned, with the recipient of the news passive-aggressively asking me why I was able to keep my job when she lost hers.

No matter how they have responded, I have tried to behave and respond as professionally and empathetically as possible until I walked them out. I shook their hands, wished them the best, and then returned to the conference room to break down in tears. I hired many of these people away from other companies and then had to eliminate their roles less than a year later. Although everyone responds differently, two things have proven to be true in every instance—the person impacted always ends up in a better place afterward, and the business figures out a way to operate effectively with fewer people. The company culture usually takes a small but significant hit, but the sun still comes up the next day. But boy, does it suck.

Layoffs are hard but inevitable. Every employee may be a financial cost to an organization, but they are also humans with real feelings who are experiencing rejection, fear, disappointment, confusion, and shame. Every person must go home and tell their wife, husband, children, parents, and roommate that they lost their job, having to face humiliation and pity. Companies have good intentions, attempting to separate the human element from the bottom line, but there are casualties. Silicon Valley legend Bill Campbell is quoted in *The Hard Thing About Hard Things* by Ben Horowitz as saying, "You cannot let him keep his job, but you absolutely can let him keep his respect." God calls us to treat people the way that we would want to be treated with empathy, authenticity, and honesty.

Following the layoffs at Rackspace, tension was definitely high. As a result, I immediately announced the consolidation of the remaining marketers into an efficient operating structure, re-defined their roles and responsibilities, key performance indicators (KPIs), and rules of engagement with other functional leaders, handed the playbook to my boss–and then I resigned.

I accepted an offer from Gartner, based on a referral from my previous CMO, Carla, for the CMO role over their Digital Markets division (GDM). Gartner was a large $4B+ IT research and insights company, and I was ecstatic about the opportunity to lead and grow the 80-person marketing team. The General Manager for GDM was looking for a high-functioning marketing leader with deep experience in building a brand while continuing to grow business performance. For the first time in my career, I would have the opportunity to manage the entire funnel, from brand to demand, in a business with a significant marketing budget that drives 100% of inbound leads.

Anytime someone resigns or considers a move to another opportunity (me included), I always think, "Are we running toward something or away from something?" It forces us to think about why we are taking the new job to ensure that our intentions and motives are pure. I accepted the job at Gartner, knowing with full certainty that I was running toward something new and exciting where I would develop my skills as a true end-to-end marketing leader, make an enormous impact on the business and my team, and thrive professionally. With the average life of a CMO at 18 months, I knew that I wanted to hit the ground running quickly. I took two weeks off and started at Gartner in April 2019. The week I left, the CEO at Rackspace was let go, and the rest of the leadership team was turned over within the next two months. I couldn't have chosen better timing. I call it a God thing. His timing is always perfect.

Story 9 Takeaways:

- **Embrace the suck.** God doesn't waste suffering. Sometimes, things happen when you least expect them, but God's plan is always perfect. It provides you with the perspective to comfort and empathize with others who are going through similar struggles.

- **Be willing to pivot.** Industries evolve and change over time. Be willing to learn new skills to thrive in declining sectors. Your ability to embrace change can lead to resilience and success.

- **Approach layoffs with empathy, authenticity, and speed.** Treat others with the respect and consideration you would want in their situation.

- **Always be running toward something great.** When considering career moves, reflect on whether you're running toward something brilliant or away from something undesirable. Ensure your decisions are about growth aligned to your goals and values rather than just avoiding something.

- **Optimize your business for efficiency.** Minimize unnecessary costs, streamline workflows, and make tough decisions that benefit both the business and the people involved.

STORY 10

Don't Be a Doormat.
Speak Up for Yourself.

Throughout my four years at Sabre from 1999 to 2003, I was fortunate enough to be promoted a few times and expand my scope. I started as a Marketing Analyst in our Airline Solutions business and then became a Product Marketing Specialist in Travel Agency Solutions. By 2002, I became a Product Manager for our point-of-sale solutions, eVoya and Turbo Sabre. I remember the day that I was promoted to Product Manager. It felt like the scene in *Top Gun* when Maverick and Goose only get selected to go to Miramar because Cougar "lost it and turned in his wings." My boss Al told me that he needed a product manager because his other PM quit, which he followed with a long diatribe about how I was too young for this job, that I wasn't ready to take on this much responsibility, but that I was the backup quarterback, and he was having to play me against the best team in town. He hated having to give the job to me, but after I recovered from the shock of his piercing words and picked my ego up off the floor, I felt determined to prove him wrong.

I was good at my job. I worked my butt off, focused on the things that mattered, and drove results. I worked smartly, without wasting time, and I was willing to put in the time and effort to learn new things. My boss was resentful of the fact that he had to give me a promotion earlier than he received that same opportunity, and his ego needed me to know and appreciate that. This was my first taste of understanding that many workplace decisions *regarding* me are not always *about* me. They are driven by business needs, manager insecurity, or just good old-fashioned timing. Regardless, I know that these opportunities are not accidental. God has a plan. He opens these doors for a reason, and it is our job to seize the moments and milk them for all they are worth. I was not his punching bag; he just needed me to be humbled at the ripe old age of 25.

Fast forward 11 years to 2013, when my boss, JT at AMD, told me that the new SVP of global business units, Lisa, wanted to talk to me about a Chief of Staff opportunity. She had heard that I was smart, hard-working, and delivered high-quality work. I was both flattered and petrified. I had never met Lisa, but she had a reputation for being extremely intelligent, very driven, and incredibly tough to work for. She had high expectations for her team and worked long hours without a lot of the warm and fuzzy. Lisa was beyond capable and well respected but feared amongst associates for her no-frills, direct style.

The speculation around the office was that Lisa would be the next CEO of AMD. Despite multiple trusted advisors telling me to run the other way, I agreed to meet with her. As a young mom of two little boys and a 6-month old baby girl, my mentors feared that I would be working around the clock and miss out on precious time with my family. However, no one disagreed that the experience would be invaluable and could change my career forever. As a perpetual optimist and someone who strives to exceed expectations and accomplish what others can't, I was intrigued by the idea of stepping up my game and proving to others that I could do it all. There is nothing I love more than winning others over (my #2 Gallup strength).

I met with Lisa, and she was lovely and encouraging. She expected the role to last 9-12 months, and then I would move back into one of the business units. I would work closely with her Executive Assistant and her Vice

President of Operations to manage her executive operations, communications, board of directors' content, organizational changes, and strategic projects. As a mid-level executive, I was given the opportunity to work for a brilliant, female, kick-ass leader who had a vision for where the company was going and the brains to back it up.

Regardless, I struggled with the decision of whether to take this role. The achiever and egomaniac in me wanted the job, but the mom and wife in me were nervous. I had never really worked for a tough, C-level leader like this before, and I wasn't sure how that beatdown would affect my emotional and mental mindset and confidence, both at work and at home. Jim and I discussed the decision at length, and he reminded me that he was my partner in this to help fill in the gaps at home. I knew this experience would be game-changing, and as part of my perpetual need to be a poster child for successful work-life balance, I saw this role as an opportunity to showcase the ability to do something big while continuing to be an engaged and attentive contributor at home. That meant that I made a promise to Jim and to myself that I would carve out time every evening to be physically, mentally, and emotionally present with my family. No phone, no email, no work between 5:30 and 8:30 p.m. Work would still be there after the kids went to bed.

Ultimately, I took the job.

In a chief of staff position, the "product" is a person, not a business. I was responsible for managing the operations and communications for a person who carried the weight of the company on her shoulders. My mind was constantly monopolized by, *What does Lisa need* or *What can I help Lisa with,* resulting in an unhealthy fear of disappointing her or letting her down. I let her opinion of me decide my worth and value in every working moment— and during the evenings and weekends as well. She had the ability to set the tone for the room, so if she was in a good mood, the meeting was great. If she wasn't, then watch out. I let my moods be dictated by hers, and I didn't know how to leave it at the office when I went home at night. My husband and kids could feel it despite my best efforts to shake it off during my commute home from work.

I respected her ability to manage a company and take it to the next level, but workdays were tough. A senior executive of a publicly traded company in the middle of a turnaround is under a lot of pressure, so she was not always kind. She told me to check my personal life at the door and that she didn't want to know anything about my family or interests outside of work. She said, "It will be much harder to fire you if I know your kids' names." Despite the politeness at the beginning of my role, the honeymoon was over. Once we got comfortable and reality kicked in, meetings were more tense, conversations were strained, and stress was high due to declining business performance. She began speaking down to me or yelling at me indirectly through her operations leader while leaving me out of critical conversations.

I also began to notice a trend about her that rang true with other strong, domineering leaders. They surround themselves with followers who are often better at executing orders than adding thoughtful, often contrasting perspectives to the team. In one instance, her right-hand operations leader pulled me aside after a meeting and said, "I saw you laugh at the beginning of the meeting before we got started. Your laughter is not welcome in our meetings. Please try to take your role more seriously."

Another time, I sent that same operations leader a draft of a communication for my boss to send out to the whole company. I said, "Can you approve, or does Lisa need to approve?"

Her response was, "No need for Lisa to approve," so I sent it out.

The next thing I knew, the operations leader was scolding me via email. *"I told you that Lisa needed to approve!"*

It turned out that what she *meant* to write was, "No *[comma]* need for Lisa to approve." It's amazing what a comma can do. *Eats, Shoots & Leaves,* I guess. Anyway, the constant berating and belittling from my boss over insignificant issues began to chip away at my self-confidence, causing me to question my own sanity and capabilities. I became increasingly afraid of my boss and her henchmen, and my larger-than-life optimism began to shrivel.

Out of fear of getting in trouble or being publicly humiliated in a meeting, I recognize now that I retreated, shrinking into myself and executing everything she asked without question or discussion, and I think she knew that she had me. She was aware that I was intelligent and capable, but she didn't show me respect, most likely because I hadn't given her a reason to. A "Yes Man" doesn't win any brownie points with a leader like this one, at least not in the long run. However, the constant unfounded scolding wore me down quickly, and I lost my ability to hold my tongue or hide my emotions. I didn't react defensively or passive-aggressively in a meeting in front of other people as I was often tempted to do. Instead, I pulled her aside into a conference room one-on-one and said something like this:

"I am smart and really good at my job. I have managed teams, led complex projects, spoken at events on behalf of this company, and executed flawlessly. Every day, I walk in here confidently at my full 5'3" with my head held high, but by 6 p.m., I crawl out of here three inches off the ground because you have kicked the sh*t out of me all day. Bring me in. Trust me. Treat me like a human. Let me do my job. I guarantee that I will do it well. But you must give me space and context to execute at full capacity."

She looked at me, stunned, as if no one had ever stood up to her, while I secretly feared for my life. But then she said, "You're right. I haven't been treating you well. I will fix it." And she did. After that, my time working for her was empowering, free, and much more positive. She had me take more ownership, included me in confidential, strategic meetings, and trusted the work that I was doing. I learned that sometimes, tough leaders just want to test you until they know that you can handle it. I think she appreciated me pushing back because she now knew that I could get in the trenches with her. Whether we liked each other or not, it didn't matter. We finally had mutual respect.

Over the next 15 months, I settled into life on the front lines of executive decision-making. I learned what senior leadership cares about, what they focus on, and how they consider options before making decisions. I saw the world differently after that experience. I observed that being highly capable and respectable is not always nice. There's a difference between managing a team and inspiring a team as a leader. I also watched and admired how Lisa always thought three steps ahead, making decisions now that no one understood in service of her long-term master vision. It was truly spectacular to watch, even if some days were hard. Like I tell my kids in sports: "You learn as much from losing as you do winning. You develop character either way." In this role, I felt like I often lost emotionally, yet I learned more mentally than I have ever learned in any other job, so I'll call that a win.

Fight for what is right, but do so in a respectful, thoughtful manner. Don't be afraid to bet on yourself when others might not. Leaders want leaders they can trust. Some managers may seem to surround themselves with doormats to feel powerful, but these leaders also know that they need strong backbones to help execute their visions and make them better. Confidence is contagious. The book *One Minute Manager* by Ken Blanchard and Spencer Johnson talks about the relationship between confidence and competence. They define competence as "a function of knowledge and skills, which can be gained from education, training, and/or experience." Confidence is "a measure of a person's self-assuredness—a feeling of being able to do a task well without much supervision." They go on to explain (and I am paraphrasing) that confidence without competence is disastrous and devastating to an organization, but competence without confidence is a waste of great talent. I was the latter, often cowering under the desk out of fear of being belittled or shamed, but I was extremely capable of doing my job. Finding my confidence by facing the inhibitor head-on became a catalyst for a substantial increase in my work product, performance, and contribution.

Story 10 Takeaways:

- **Tackle the obstacles.** Even if situations seem challenging, confront adversity as an opportunity to learn, adapt, and come out stronger on the other side. Extract insights and knowledge from tough experiences that will help you grow professionally and personally.

- **Disconnect daily.** When considering career moves, make sure you have support at home and block significant time every day to disconnect and be completely present with your family. Seek to strike a balance between achieving your professional goals and maintaining important family values. If they are in conflict, make a change.

- **Stand up for your worth and value.** Don't be a passive participant in your career journey. Advocate for yourself, address concerns, and seek the respect you deserve. Believe in your skills and capabilities. Open, honest communication can lead to better understanding, improved relationships, and a healthier work environment.

- **Strive for mutual respect with your leaders.** Push back when necessary, but do so professionally and thoughtfully. Demonstrate that you can handle challenges. Holding your ground can earn you respect.

- **Be both competent and confident.** Being capable at your job is important, but having the confidence to assert yourself, take on challenges, and communicate effectively is critical for allowing your competence to shine.

Joy at Work Can Affect Your Leadership Style.

In 2015, I got a call from my friend Dave, who was running corporate communications at Rackspace. Dave worked at AMD in the past but left a couple of years prior, and now he wanted to establish a brand management capability at Rackspace. I was very familiar with Rackspace because my dad was in business with the father of the company's founder, Graham Weston. Rackspace was another move toward a smaller company, about half the size of AMD at that time, which aligned with my career vision to eventually move to a startup.

Rackspace was a managed hosting company that was expanding into the managed cloud services space as they were forced to differentiate with the rise of public cloud powerhouses like Amazon Web Services, Google Cloud, and Microsoft Azure. Everyone who went to the Rack loved it, as the corporate culture was unmatched, and I was excited about the possibility of getting back into marketing. This felt like the perfect step for me.

I immediately fell in love with Rackspace and carried great pride in being a Racker. Before one's start date, all Rackers complete the Gallup Strengths assessment to stack rank their strengths from 1 to 34. The belief at Rackspace, as I understood it, was that the return on investment (ROI) by doubling down on strengths far exceeded the return on fixing weaknesses. My top six strengths were:

- Achiever
- Woo (Winning Others Over)
- Communication
- Positivity
- Maximizer
- Responsibility

The top five were listed on my ID badge, and these strengths showed up in every conversation. Rackers would often lean over and look at their colleague's badges and say something like, "Oh, you're an Arranger. Would you be willing to pull in all the relevant parties that are needed to execute this project?" Or "Since you are both an Achiever and have high Responsibility, I know you will go home and try to finish this tonight. Take your time, and let's shoot for an update next week." Rackers took their core values very seriously by treating each other as friends and family, taking interpersonal issues directly to the Racker rather than escalating, and focusing on delivering substance over flash.

I came into Rackspace in 2015, deflated from the daily beatdown I felt at AMD. At that time, AMD was the losing party in both the graphics and computer processing duopolies against Nvidia and Intel, respectively. The daily grind as an underdog working for the leader in charge of turning that ship around was a stressful and high-pressure environment. Fortunately, AMD pivoted the business and accelerated far beyond the competition, with their stock rising above $150 (which I am a little bitter about since I sold out at $1.80 in 2015). However, for me, after a year and a half in the chief of staff seat, I was ready for a change. I saw behind the curtain and knew too much.

For my own mental health, I needed to be a part of something where people truly loved their jobs and each other, a culture that valued respect, transparency, and authenticity. I found it in Rackspace, but I realized very quickly that I needed to work through the funk that I still carried from my previous role. I went into AMD with a Myers Briggs profile of ENFP (Extraverted, Intuitive, Feeling, Prospecting), which is often referred to as the Campaigner. According to 16personalities.com, a Campaigner "tends to embrace big ideas and actions that reflect their sense of hope and goodwill toward others. Their vibrant energy can flow in many directions." They are often seen as "outgoing, openhearted, and open-minded with a lively, upbeat approach to life, yet always longing for meaningful, emotional connections with other people."

After working in the chief of staff capacity at AMD, my profile took a major pivot, and I became an ESTJ (Extraverted, Sensing, Thinking, Judging), with my only remaining constant being extraversion. According to 16personalities.com, this profile is known as the Executive, "Possessing great fortitude, emphatically following their own sensible judgment. They often serve as a stabilizing force among others, able to offer solid direction amid adversity." I took on my boss' profile type, representing tradition and order while abandoning my own feelings and emotions. I liked that I had grown into an Executive, proving my ability to scale up and lead, but I lost who I was at the core somewhere along the way. I wasn't the same person as I was before Lisa, but I wasn't Lisa either. I needed to rediscover who I was, and Rackspace provided the perfect warm, embracing culture to find me again.

The Rackspace office was the visual embodiment of the fantastic culture I was so happy to be walking into. Graham bought the old Windsor Park Mall in San Antonio, where I used to shop as a kid with my mom and turned it into the company's headquarters. He converted it into an open floor plan office with themed neighborhoods like the Toy Shoppe, which took the place of the old Dillard's, where all the conference rooms were named after common kid toys like "Tinker Toys" or "Russian Dolls." One of my favorite rooms was the Doll House, which had an external facade and front porch just like a white,

Victorian doll house and was furnished with antique furniture, leather couches, and classic wallpaper. Like all good tech companies in the early 2000s, Rackspace had ping pong tables, a slide from the 2nd floor, and a plethora of lounge seating to work, chat, or relax throughout the day. The office in the San Antonio community of Windsor was affectionately called "The Castle" because Graham's parents met at the Queen of England's wedding to Prince Phillip at Windsor Castle.

The one major challenge with Rackspace was that it was in San Antonio while I lived in Austin. Graham believed that he could hang on to better tech talent if his company was the primary technology game in town rather than trying to compete with other big tech companies or start-ups in Silicon Valley or even Austin. However, once most of the talent in San Antonio was picked over, Rackspace began recruiting in Austin, which was about 90 minutes away. To solve that commute challenge, Rackspace offered a shuttle four days a week that included Wi-Fi, tables, and comfortable seating. Rackers essentially had a mobile office as they were driven down IH-35 at 70 miles an hour. This allowed me the flexibility to work remotely a couple of days a week and ride the shuttle to "The Castle" the other days, giving me some control over my schedule and preparation for the COVID-19 lockdown a few years later.

Throughout my four-and-a-half years at Rackspace, I had an incredible run of interesting projects, expanded scope, and progressive responsibility and growth, serving as a leader and executive in a company experiencing massive transformation. I learned to appreciate and respect diversity in a completely different way. Up until this point, I thought of diversity as related only to ethnicity and gender, and I always pushed to bring the broadest perspectives and ideas to the team. But, as I managed a team of designers, writers, and brand strategists, I began to appreciate and witness a completely different take on diversity, such as the value of extraverts versus introverts, creatives versus businesspeople, planners versus those who operate best under a time crunch.

As an extravert who makes decisions very quickly, I would lead a staff meeting and say something like, "I had an idea for this new project," followed by my perspective and then, "Everyone good with that? Great! Let's do it." I quickly learned from Royce, one of my brilliant, introverted designers—who pulled me aside to share that some folks (like him) needed time to digest the information, think through it, and then come back with their feedback—that my style might not be universal. Of course, that was fine with me, but it never crossed my mind because I was blinded by the way that I process.

In another instance, one of the leaders on my team would always wait until the last minute to get his projects done. It drove me crazy, but as a former newscaster, he thrived under the stress and ticking clock of knowing he was going live in less than ten minutes. It helped that his work was always perfection. I had to let go and trust that he would get it done on time (and not one minute sooner). I have since tried to create a space where different approaches are encouraged to thrive and where my team feels comfortable calling me out when I forget.

I started at Rackspace as a Director of Brand in a managed hosting company for small businesses and helped partner with executives and customers to reframe our positioning as a managed cloud service provider for upper mid-market and enterprise customers. I was promoted to Senior Director after a year and increased my purview beyond brand and creative to include content, campaigns, and go-to-market strategy. Two years later, our Chief Product Officer asked me to move to the Product team to set up a solutions capability and product marketing center of excellence. I was promoted to Vice President and given the freedom and flexibility to establish vertical marketing capabilities and build out a team of star performers from various industries. In that role, I was asked to become the Austin office site leader in addition to my day job.

The Austin office grew over time and needed strong, female, local leadership, given that most of the executive team was in San Antonio. This freed me up to stay in Austin more often rather than commute to San Antonio and exposed me to additional operational and cultural experiences cross-functionally. I led quarterly town halls for the Austin office, helped facilitate office events for employee engagement, and organized volunteer outings in the area for Austin Rackers. Rackspace gave me a chance to experience significant marketing and leadership growth and helped solidify my expertise and credibility as a technology executive.

I had an incredible and fulfilling run at Rackspace—one of my favorites of my entire career—as I experienced so much in a culture that loved its people. A great example of that was a handwritten card I received from Louis Alterman, Chief Financial Officer, when I was promoted to Vice President. The note said, *"I'm thrilled to get to congratulate you on your well-deserved promotion. To be a Vice President at Rackspace is a major accomplishment and something to be proud of."* I had never received a personal note like that written on real stationery from a senior executive. I still have that note. Another time, my boss, Carla, and I carpooled the 70 miles to work together from Austin to San Antonio. A ladder flew out of the back of the truck in front of us as we were traveling full speed down I-35. My boss slammed on her brakes, threw her right arm across my chest like I was her lion cub, and navigated quickly and safely to avoid the ladder. Her instinct was to protect me. When my son had an emergency appendectomy, my Rackspace team sent a huge stuffed animal and cookie basket to him in the hospital. I always felt loved and cared for at Rackspace.

By the end of my tenure at Rackspace, my Myers Briggs profile had found its happy place, combining the perspective and leadership I experienced with the person I was wired to be at the core. I was an ENFJ (Extraverted, Intuitive, Feeling, and Judging), known as the Protagonist, and I have remained there ever since. 16personalities.com describes the protagonists as "warm, forthright types who love helping others and tend to have strong ideas and values. They back their perspective with the creative energy to achieve their goals. They often feel called to serve a greater purpose in life, striving to have a positive impact on other people and the world around them. They are born leaders." I was no longer the shadow of another leader. I discovered a joy through work and through leadership, knowing that my identity was in the God who created me, and I would build confidence in forging my own path, operating with a sense of purpose and not a blueprint created by someone else. I knew what God called me to do, which was to love Him and love others, and I finally tapped into how to glorify Him and treat others well through my leadership position. There was freedom in knowing who I was and why I was here. I just needed the time and experience to trust myself and the faith to trust the One who brought me there.

Story 11 Takeaways:

- **Connect your work to your values.** Seek out workplace cultures that align with your beliefs and contribute to your overall well-being.

- **Embrace your strengths.** The return on your investment will be far greater than trying to fix your weaknesses. Building on your strengths will allow you to excel in the right role, leading to greater fulfillment at work and more effective leadership.

- **Adapt as your career progresses.** Your personality and leadership style will evolve over time based on your experiences and environments. Embrace your authentic self in your leadership role. Being genuine and confident in your own expertise can inspire trust and respect from your team.

- **Cultivate a diverse environment.** It's not just about ethnicity, gender, and orientation. Seek to understand different perspectives, work styles, and approaches within your team. Tailor your communication style to accommodate various personality types and create an environment where individuals feel confident sharing their full selves.

Speak With a Period, Not a Question Mark.

A fellow female executive once asked me a question, and before I could answer, she said, "No is an acceptable answer." Then she followed with, "And 'No' is a complete sentence." I loved this, especially as a woman who often feels the need to explain or disclaim every response. Sometimes we, as women, are our own worst enemy. Media-driven stereotypes and fictional characters on TV have long trained women about how we are "supposed" to behave in professional situations. Specifically, that we are responsible for making others feel comfortable and valued over ourselves. We are also wired differently—we have a need and desire to be liked that sometimes overshadows our need and desire to be respected and taken seriously. It's a fine balance to be the cheerleader, the organizer, and the badass leader all at the same time. Striking that balance, I think, begins with paying attention to the way we communicate.

One of the ladies on my team, Sharon, at Rackspace, taught me the word "uptalk." I wasn't familiar with this term, but I have certainly witnessed the concept over and over. "Uptalk" is defined by Oxford Languages as "a manner of speaking in which declarative sentences are uttered with rising intonation at the end, as if they were questions." Essentially, uptalk is the way that some people (most often women) present innovative ideas as a means of suggestion or question—rather than a declaration or directive—so that they don't offend anyone or come across as too aggressive. Instead, they often end their statement with a question mark and then proceed to caveat the suggestion with a bunch of "I think" and "Maybe we should consider" instead of speaking in facts the way that men often do.

A woman might say, "I was thinking that maybe we could try expanding our target market. That might help us get more traction if you guys think that would be a good idea?"

A man's version would say something like, "We need a bigger target market. Let's get the research together and execute next quarter."

Suddenly, we hear this directive from a male that sounds like a big decision has been made, yet we are in a state of discussing and considering the risks and concerns of the female's position.

As women who support other women, we have a responsibility offline after a meeting to call our women counterparts out and encourage them to own those ideas. Speak with a big fat exclamation point, not a question mark. When women uptalk, they are undermining their own ideas by presenting risk and a lack of confidence that might not otherwise be observed by the audience. We are convincing our stakeholders not to take us seriously because we fear they won't like us or our ideas. We want to be team players and collaborators, so an exclamation point implies power and singular-direction communication rather than partnership and bi-directional discussion. That's what makes us amazing at being women, but it also delays our progress at the executive table.

As a female, I am guilty of this sometimes as well. Our credibility is not built entirely in that room. Our hard work, strong performance results, and experience add gravitas to our comments, so we don't need to be aggressive and cold-hearted in the way we communicate. We just need to trust that our opinion, delivered with confidence and authority, is backed by expertise and a proven track record that doesn't require any caveats or second-guessing. I have learned not to undermine my own mind, but it's a work in progress.

Story 12 Takeaways:

- **Speak with conviction and confidence.** Avoid using uptalk, which can undermine the strength of your words. Present with gravitas and build credibility through your hard work, achievements, and performance impact.

- **Don't overcompensate for success by weakening your communication.** Present your ideas assertively. Use declarative sentences rather than turning them into questions. Avoid over-explanation by delivering your point succinctly and clearly. "No" is a complete sentence.

- **Balance collaboration and authority.** You can be a team player while also projecting confidence, approachability, and leadership in your communication.

- **Challenge stereotypes.** Don't believe everything you see on TV that may affect the way you think you are expected to behave in professional situations. Focus instead on being respected and taken seriously while being true to yourself.

Set Boundaries and Protect Your Non-negotiables.

I went to work for Dell in 2009 when my oldest son, Vann, was 12 months old. Before I accepted the position, I took a calculated risk and asked my boss, Margaret, if I could leave work by 4:15 p.m. every day. I told her that I would arrive early, work hard all day, leave early, and then log back in late at night for an hour or two to catch up from the day. Vann was awake between 5 and 8 p.m., and I wanted to be a part of that time with him. Nothing that I did at 4:30 or 5 p.m. couldn't be done at 8 or 9 p.m. instead. As a fairly new mom, this was the first time I had ever put myself in that position of publicizing a certain mom vs. career trade-off. Fortunately, Margaret accepted the request without hesitation. I learned very quickly to always understand and communicate my non-negotiables early and often but back them up with hard work and trust building. My new boss didn't know anything about me or my work ethic at this point, but by believing in myself and my work product enough, I had the courage to ask for what was important to me. With this new arrangement in place, God slowly managed my "mom guilt," assuring me that I could thrive at both being a mother and making an impact in the office.

I was working as a Product Line Manager at Dell on the Latitude commercial client business. Unlike any other job that I have had since then, I never found my footing at Dell to understand how my work contributed to the overall corporate strategy. Dell is a huge organization spread across multiple cities, buildings, functions, and business units, so that Google Earth view of the corporate structure never became clear to me. My job was fine. I liked the people, and the work was manageable, if not inspiring. However, in this season, "fine" was perfect for me as I was balancing a long commute, trying to raise a baby boy, and finding a home in Austin. I have learned that it is okay to balance career excitement and ambition with the season of life. With a young baby at home, I wasn't looking to change the world or lead a large team. I was happy to do a smaller job well rather than push for a bigger job that would stretch me, knowing that the most significant role for me at that time was being a new mom in a new city. I believe that we can give ourselves permission to make big bets on different aspects of our lives and that they may vary based on where we are on our journey. It is absolutely a marathon, not a sprint, so I was so thankful for that opportunity at Dell to give me big tech experience while I reveled in this mom thing.

When Vann was 19 months old and about seven months into my career at Dell, we found out that we were pregnant with baby number two. A few months later, my boss, Margaret, left Dell and went to AMD to lead Integrated Marketing. She called me and asked if I would be interested in joining her at AMD, working on the brand portfolio. My relocation contract at Dell was just about to expire, so I took her up on the opportunity. I was seven months pregnant by this point and very clearly showing. (I make large babies, and at only 5'3" tall, those babies show early.) I walked into my interview with John, the Vice President of Corporate Brand, and he tried so hard to be professional. He didn't take his eyes off of mine and refused to look down, which I appreciated but also found pretty funny. I figured that it was a long shot to get hired into a new role right before I went out on maternity leave, but John and I clicked, and he offered me the job as the Sr. Manager of Brand.

I learned through that experience that we should always bring our whole selves into the workplace, that we shouldn't apologize for our personal lives as a liability, and that quality leaders will hire the best person for the job, regardless of personal circumstances. Hiring is a long game and shouldn't be limited by short-term obstacles like delayed start dates or maternity leaves. Find the right candidate, and don't let the logistics interfere.

A few years later, I did an exercise in a leadership class where I put together a line graph mapping major milestones in my life to the highs and lows of my emotional state at that time. The x-axis was years from birth to present day, and the y-axis was a range for my emotional happiness on a scale of 1 to 10. I mapped one line for personal and the other for professional. The irony is that oftentimes, when my *professional* was at a high, my *personal* was at a low (and vice versa). Sometimes when we lean so far into work or career development, we see our personal lives plummet. When we are experiencing the highest highs of our real life (marriage, babies, travel), our work may take a backseat. I guess the ultimate goal is to figure out how to build a satisfying and successful career that doesn't require too much personal sacrifice or at least be willing to live with the tradeoffs.

A few years later at Rackspace, that tradeoff conversation became a reality again. I was managing a team of 6 brand managers, designers, and creatives. My CMO, Carla, asked me out to coffee and offered me a promotion to expand my scope to include all central marketing. This would give me my first opportunity to manage a large, multi-level team of 25-30 marketers and make a much more significant impact on business performance. Oftentimes, leaders will ask you nicely to take on additional responsibility as a compliment to your capabilities, but they won't follow that up with additional compensation or a bigger title. And most of the time, we as women (and often as pleasers) take those additional responsibilities out of both flattery and in hopes of it leading to something bigger. That was not the case this time. Carla was willing to do it all for me—money, title, scope—because she believed in me and my ability to grow and scale.

I turned her down. I had 3 small kids at home, and I made plenty of money (in my mind) to pay the bills. I have always wanted enough money to survive, give back, pay for college, save a little, and provide my family with the fairly conservative lifestyle that we wanted, but I never needed any more than that. I told her, "No, thank you. I am home every night with my kids, I never miss any of their football games or piano recitals, and I can manage my team well within working hours. If I can do all of that, then I am fine to stay at this level at least until my kids graduate from high school." She was shocked. (She later told me that I looked at her "as if she just handed me a bag of sh*t.") I was so protective and grateful for my position as a hands-on mom with a thriving career, rather than a career woman who happened to have kids, that I didn't want to mess that up. My time management and personal priorities were perfectly aligned.

A few days later, she asked me again, and I turned her down again for all the same reasons. Finally, she just came to me a third time and said, "I promoted you and gave you a raise. You are the only person I want for this team and this bigger responsibility. And I promise you that I will protect your time. I will make sure you are home every night, and I will ensure you aren't pulled into late-night meetings. I won't make you choose between your career and your family."

She believed in me—even more than I believed in myself—yet she respected my boundaries. By being vocal about my non-negotiables and, of course, putting in the hard work during the day every day leading up to that moment, my boss trusted me, pushed for me, and gave me opportunities that I didn't even ask for. As a mother herself, she saw so much potential in where I could be in my career yet still be very present with my family at home. She saw me as a whole person, not just as a worker or marketer, and she architected an opportunity where I could be successful in all aspects of my life. I take that story with me everywhere I go as I try to pay that forward to the teams that I manage.

Now, in every new role, I make it very clear to my boss that "I don't miss my kids' games…ever." That is my one unbreakable rule to protect those special, fleeting moments and milestones with my family. That is my nonnegotiable.

In that role, as the Senior Director of Integrated Marketing at Rackspace, I had an opportunity to build and lead our very first brand awareness campaign. Carla gave me her full support to dream big and go for it. My team and I wrote a very detailed campaign brief based on shifting our positioning in the market and establishing a new category for managed multi-cloud services. We conducted an agency Request for Proposal (RFP), found a brilliant creative and media agency, selected a couple of leading creative concepts, tested them with our target market to see if they shifted consideration and preference for the brand, and then predicted a return on investment at various spend levels.

Carla made the call that we keep the project and content to a small group, not for secrecy reasons, but to limit the opinions and avoid the common pitfall of neutering good creative by trying to satisfy too many perspectives on a seemingly subjective topic. Once we were ready, we compiled the whole story and pitch deck and took it to the Executive Leadership Team (ELT) with one primary objective—to secure $15M in brand spend to double unaided brand awareness from 6% to 12% within 12 months. We warned the ELT that they would not see pipeline growth immediately, so we needed their commitment to continue the campaign for at least 12 months. Brand spend is a long game, so we needed to set expectations that they wouldn't see real pipeline expansion for 8-10 months and that sales cycles should shorten with brand awareness over that same period. We communicated with authority and expertise, instilling confidence in the ELT that this was a solid investment and that we were the right team to lead it. We received ELT approval, followed by financial support from the Board of Directors in less than 30 minutes, causing my boss to give me the "When Pigs Fly" award for making something huge happen that had never been done before at Rackspace.

We launched a couple of months later and doubled our unaided brand awareness within seven months, beating our goal by five months. By empowering me to own my function and keeping our trust circle small, my core team and I were able to create and protect provocative creative that tested well and delivered results without the dilution of too many opinions. We held true to the brand, and the brand won.

Story 13 Takeaways:

- **Be crystal clear on your non-negotiables.** You might not get the job, but the alternative is worse. Sacrificing what is important to you is not worth that job. Negotiate for balance and communicate your needs confidently. Then back them up with hard work and trust building.

- **Set boundaries that align with your priorities.** And don't apologize for them. Success is not purely defined in the workplace. Put a value on the comprehensive success of career plus personal that allows the combination to thrive.

- **Keep your trust circle small.** When working on creative projects or making major life decisions, too many opinions will dilute the integrity and intent. Motivations vary from person to person, so stay true to the vision.

STORY 14

Women Are a Gift, Even if We're a Pain in the Butt Sometimes.

It wasn't always harmless fun in elementary school as I pushed boundaries, trying to figure out who I was. One day, in 3rd grade, three of my girlfriends and I were doing the "monkee walk" around the playground, singing a version of that famous song about two of our friends: "Nicole and Jason sitting in a tree. F-U-C-K-I-N-G."

Can you imagine?

We were 8 years old! We didn't even know what that word meant, but we looked up to see our teacher, Mrs. Schwab, staring at us. We were immediately sent to the principal's office, reprimanded mercilessly, and asked to stand along the wall at recess for the whole week. Since my mom was a teacher in the district, I was petrified that she would find out and I would be in huge trouble at home. Somehow, though, she never did. I told her and my dad the story in my late 20s (once I was sure the statute of limitations had run out), and we all had a huge laugh. I am not a mean person, I don't tell lies, and I don't say cuss words ever, but I can honestly say that second and third grade were my rebellious years in all three areas. I am thankful to have worked most of that out of my system at an early age.

Fortunately, throughout the rest of my life, women have mostly proven to be a true gift. At four months pregnant with my first son, I started playing golf with a group of ladies from Kraft every Tuesday morning at 6:30 a.m. We would play nine holes at a links course called Tam O'Shanter in Chicago and then head into the office and get ready for the day. It turns out that pregnant ladies are pretty decent golfers, according to an LPGA golf instructor, as the belly forced my hands into the right position. In the fall of that year, my group of golfing ladies was asked to play in a golf tournament that Kraft sponsored at Twin Creek Country Club. Famous LPGA star Paula Creamer, who was dressed in pink from head to toe, spoke to everyone before we teed off in a scramble format. Our foursome was matched up with an LPGA pro who rode with us all day and gave us tips at every hole on ways to prevent a slice, how to read the green, how to shift if the ball is on an uphill versus downhill lie, and how to adjust for slope and direction. I can't name the pro who helped us, but I still, to this day, think about those golf tips every time I play.

I kept up my golf game as my pregnancy would allow, but eventually, I hung up my clubs only when my belly grew so large it became more of an obstruction than an advantage. Those golf outings on Tuesday mornings were my first taste of working with a tight group of cross-functional female leaders whom I knew would have my back in the office. Building a personal relationship outside of work helped solidify trust inside the workplace. Women get a bad reputation for backstabbing each other, but throughout most of my experience, I have been blessed with strong women who want to build up other intelligent and capable women. Don't get me wrong. Female competitiveness and insecurities can get in the way sometimes. I often joke that I love a company that values smart, resilient women and puts them in leadership positions as long as I don't have to work with any of them. I say that in jest about the handful of complicated women I have worked with, but in general, I have been very fortunate to work with intelligent, collaborative, ambitious ladybosses who want to support each other.

A few years later, on my last day as Lisa's chief of staff at AMD, her Executive Assistant (EA), Pat, who became a very close friend during my tenure in the role, pulled me aside to tell me how much she would miss me after I left. Pat and I had spent hours together every day, fighting the same battles and crying through the same challenges. We had been at war together, and our bond could not be broken. She told me that every time she leaves a company or changes roles, she carries a couple of people with her as pebbles in her pocket, those precious relationships that continue long after a job change. I was thankful for Pat as she had been deep in the trenches with me every single day, and I would never forget her.

I often reflect on the pebbles in my pocket from every career move. I don't remember many of the projects I worked on or the business results that I was a part of, but I clearly remember the people with whom I was blessed to work with. These were precious souls who would listen to my venting over coffee every day, the ones who would empathize with me about every nuance inside the organization. I was able to speak shorthand with them because they knew everything that was going on. Sometimes, it was hard to bring those elements to life in full context with our loved ones outside of work, so those special pebbles inside were a lifesaver. These were the people who threw you a goodbye lunch when you resigned and helped carry your stuff to the car on your last day of work. These were the faces I thought about when I considered leaving an organization because those relationships became so vital for emotional survival between 8 a.m. and 5 p.m.

Hold tight to these people. We only get a couple at every company, so stay in touch with them, protect those relationships, and find ways to work with them again. The Lord puts people in our path for a reason. When we look back over our careers, those are the memories we will cherish the most.

My favorite crew of female leaders emerged from my time at Rackspace. Like most of the tech industry, Rackspace was a male-dominated environment, and I had to learn how to navigate the boys' club that surrounded me. I was able to be successful as a female executive, but I witnessed the men having sidebars and backdoor promotions that women were often excluded from. Despite the daily frustrations of a small minority of chauvinistic and egotistical men, I found my tribe of women who will rule the world one day. They were brilliant, emotionally intelligent, kind, capable studs who crossed finance, marketing, human resources, operations, legal, sales, and product.

In all fairness to the male sidebars, my fierce group of fellow female executives were doing the opposite and secretly plotting our own takeover. I guess all's fair in the game as long as we knew that we were, in fact, playing a game. The biggest mistake was just being surprised by it. Our "Ladies Who Launch" group got together often to vent our complaints, encourage each other, and role-play how we would have handled the same situations differently as women versus our male counterparts. I have full confidence that if a few of these women—Rachel, Ashley, Joanna, and myself—came together to start a company, any company, we would achieve world domination. There was power in the trust, intelligence, and competency of the right formidable women.

We are different from men, and that is a beautiful thing, but we can also learn something from men in the way that they are able to compartmentalize feedback. I have observed that women want feedback conceptually because that's how we get better, but in reality, we often consume negative professional feedback as an attack on our character. We feel the need to defend our position or make excuses for our actions to prove that we are capable and that there was a rational thoughtfulness for why we made that decision. I have been guilty of this many times. I think women executives carry the weight of females everywhere, feeling the need to protect our gender's under-indexed representation. The challenge is when that exchange occurs between two women. It often gets very heated, defensive, and contentious quickly, widening a gap that was most likely very narrow to begin with. We are our own worst enemy when forced to go head-to-head, yet the presence of a contingency of well-rounded women on the leadership team has proven to be a game-changer for organizations.

Proverbs 31 describes the ideal woman as strong, respectable, wise, kind, and has a sense of humor. But she is also a capitalist with a servant's heart and takes care of her household while working hard and earning her rewards. For fear of taking any part out of context, here are just a few verses (24-27) that I love:

> *She makes linen garments and sells them;*
> *she delivers sashes to the merchant.*
> *Strength and dignity are her clothing,*
> *and she laughs at the time to come.*
> *She opens her mouth with wisdom,*
> *and the teaching of kindness is on her tongue.*
> *She looks well to the ways of her household*
> *and does not eat the bread of idleness.*

Women are called to balance the daily grind of work and home, kindness, strength, dignity, and humor, but what a gift to get to carry that burden.

Story 14 Takeaways:

- **Support other women.** As you rise, lift others up with you. Celebrate their achievements and contribute to a culture of collaboration and empowerment. Cherish relationships over projects or results.

- **Emulate the qualities of a Proverbs 31 woman.** Be strong, respectable, wise, kind, and humorous. Balance work, home, and personal growth. Own your position as a ladyboss while appreciating and learning from the strengths of your male and female counterparts.

- **Compartmentalize feedback.** Learn to distinguish between functional performance reviews and personal character attacks. Everyone has development areas, but that doesn't make us unworthy.

Know Your Value. Don't Apologize for it.

In late 2019, less than a year into my tenure at Gartner, our Chief Content Officer left the company. I never quite understood why marketing and content were separate, but he and I had partnered well together regardless. In preparation for his departure, my boss asked me to absorb the content function into my team. The content team had 35 people and needed transformation from a research and writing team to a content marketing organization. Adding content to my daily responsibilities would significantly increase my scope and workload, increasing my team from 80 to 115 people.

This was one of those moments where I was so flattered to be asked that I didn't take the risk of requesting additional compensation for the increased responsibilities. Like so many women in this position, I believed that if I asked for more money, I might jeopardize the opportunity or that my boss Ken might think poorly of me, seeing me as an opportunist rather than a team player.

As a woman in a leadership position, I should expect to be valued by the people around me, but I should also feel empowered to ask for what I deserve in case they forget. This was a stark reminder of the importance of asking for what I wanted from the very beginning. I can't just be pleased by the idea that I was invited to do more; I must communicate what I am worth. This one is hard for me because the world tells me that money and power are the ultimate measures of success. However, the Bible (my truth) says that *"success is obedience to God, empowered by the Spirit of God, motivated by love for God, and directed toward the advancement of the kingdom of God. Success begins with obeying God's command to repent and believe in Jesus Christ."* (Mark 1:15; Acts 19:4, 20:21) The rest will follow.

I often struggle with the balance between worldly ambition versus obedience to God, trying to avoid becoming a doormat yet still respecting authority (Romans 13). In the book of Luke, Chapter 9, Jesus says, *"If anyone would come after me, let him deny himself and take up his cross daily and follow me."* The reward is unconditional joy in this life and eternal life in heaven.

In the end, I ultimately decided that addressing the organizational challenges was more urgent (not more important) than satisfying my compensation adjustments. I dove headfirst into honoring and delivering the job I had been given, building out the content marketing strategy, restructuring the team, and laying off a few individuals who didn't have roles in the new organization. Ken was ecstatic with the changes and the corresponding results that followed.

I let the dust settle for a couple of weeks before I approached him with the words that I had been dreading. I practiced my conversation with him over and over, but when the time came, I could barely get the words out. It felt almost foolish after so much time, but I waited so that I could ask him face-to-face. I muttered something like, "I took on a lot of added responsibility and implemented significant organizational changes. It would be great if you could compensate me for the increased workload." It took everything I had to say those words. Ken agreed enthusiastically and confirmed that he would reconcile the compensation without committing to anything specific. However, I had to wait for the next compensation cycle, which was coming a couple of months later, in April 2020.

One month later, in March 2020, after receiving a generous compensation increase commitment in writing, the world stopped when COVID-19 was declared a global pandemic. Every company in the world hustled to figure out how to respond and adjust to the reality of the situation. Recession seemed imminent, so for Gartner, that meant no compensation increases for a while, including mine. I understood the business uncertainty, but I felt foolish for taking the job without asking for compensation from the beginning. However, I also felt gratitude for getting the opportunity to grow and nurture the newly added content team during a time of so much change and unchartered territory.

Six months later, once the COVID implications were more settled, additional limited budget became available to retain key talent in the midst of the growing "Great Resignation" era. Again, I assumed that my boss would remember his commitment to me from just a few short months prior. I didn't want to have to remind him because I believed that great work spoke for itself. In the end, Ken didn't remember nor prioritize fulfilling that commitment and making things right. I was angry, both at him and myself. I struggled with understanding if I handled anything the right way. How could I have advocated better for myself? How could I get comfortable asking for what I thought I deserved when I was desperately trying to focus on the Godly prize, not the worldly one? We must know the value that we bring to the market, and we don't need to apologize for expecting that. Write down your strengths and differentiation versus other candidates with similar skill sets. Define your value proposition. Believe in what you bring to the table. Fight for what is right. Don't apologize for it.

Ultimately, despite any frustrations or resentment from my compensation woes, I adored my time at Gartner. That first-time CMO experience in an online marketplace with significant marketing investment and resources became a pivotal moment in my understanding, appreciation, and passion for leading marketing organizations full-funnel, from brand to demand. Only when speaking to fellow CMOs, did I realize what a gift that opportunity truly was. I was able to directly influence and carry the responsibility for revenue rather than contribute leads to a sales cycle as marketers typically do. I was able to manage a house of brands that each had their own unique positioning and personality, providing the opportunity to test and learn different strategies across each property. I was blessed to have my entire team in-house, with more than 40 digital marketers who taught me the technical nuances and levers of paid media, SEO, and affiliate partnerships. Consuming and influencing that much breadth and depth of modern marketing was transformational in the way that I understood the entire discipline. In the end, Gartner represented another monumental career pivot in my perspective on marketing and leadership.

Story 15 Takeaways:

- **Know your worth.** Understand your value and the contribution you bring to the table. Be able to specify your key differentiation, unique value proposition, and proven impact.

- **Communicate your value, don't apologize for it.** Don't hesitate to ask for what you deserve, especially when taking on additional responsibilities. Overcome the fear of being seen as opportunistic by communicating your worth confidently.

- **Understand your definition of success.** Strive to balance worldly ambition with obedience to your values and beliefs.

- **Get the job done first.** While compensation is important, fulfilling your responsibilities and delivering value for the company takes precedence.

STORY 16

The Average CMO Has a Short Shelf Life.

As of now, I have been a CMO at three different technology companies over the last five years. That's an average of 20 months each. I've read studies showing 28-40 months on average, but most B2B technology CMOs I know will wholeheartedly agree that 18-24 months is the magic number. There is a reason.

Since my career started in 1999, the longest I have ever been in a single role is about 24 months. That doesn't mean that I have hopped companies every two years. It means that I have changed positions—either expanded responsibilities, received a promotion, or made a lateral transition to another function at the same company—or I have changed companies. I had three different roles at Sabre in four years, four roles at AMD in five years, and four roles at Rackspace in four years. I am a builder. I love to start a new role, assess the situation, build out the team, implement an operating model, and begin executing. After 18 months, once the team is functioning at scale, I often get bored and ready to try something new. Fortunately, that's about when my leaders recognized an opportunity and asked me to start something new. Unfortunately, there's nowhere else to go as a CMO unless I want to be a CEO, move to another company as a CMO, or do something completely different. It's the C-suite, which is typically the goal, so where do we go from there?

In addition, marketing is typically considered to be "easy" by other C-level executives. Just run some cool ads and get customers to click on them, right? That means that when business challenges arise, marketing is typically the scapegoat. The pipeline isn't growing fast enough, so marketing must not be doing its job. The reality is that there could be a product-market fit issue, or sales is not equipped to convert marketing leads into revenue. But that is more complicated, so CEOs will typically start coming up with their own marketing ideas, which they don't often know how to execute effectively. CMOs recognize that most of those ideas won't have a positive ROI – billboards, sponsorship, expensive paid advertising – but pushback creates tension that typically results in a CMO getting replaced. If a CMO doesn't have a backbone or data to prove that the investment is a bad idea, then CMOs execute their CEO's whims, cost the company a lot of money, and ultimately result in a CMO getting replaced anyway. It can be a transient job.

In a start-up with Founder CEOs, the tenure is most likely even shorter. The biggest lesson I have learned working in founder-led organizations is that the CEO is the lead marketer for the company. That means that the CMO is second in line, often leading to frustration for CMOs where they must walk the fine line between standing strong on their marketing expertise and serving as an amiable lieutenant to the CEO. That relationship only works if there is mutual respect and trust in each other's perspective and experience. Otherwise, CMOs at start-ups contribute significantly to bringing down that average tenure. In that case, it makes you wonder why CMOs ever join start-ups because they almost never make it to the big payout that is promised upon company exit three or four years later.

A fellow CMO friend of mine just left her company and started her own fractional CMO consultancy. When I reached out to her to find out the story, this is what she replied: *"I craved a seat at the table for so many years, but when I finally got to the table, it was a boy's club or a club that didn't respect a marketing leader's opinion. All I wanted to do was create value and just do good marketing for companies, but instead, I always felt trapped and defensive."*

Marketing is the classic scapegoat. Being a CMO requires thick skin. Be willing to defend marketing best practices by measuring everything that can be tracked. Be flexible but stand up to naysayers who question marketing decisions. Data is king. The battle between marketing and sales is a tale as old as time, but it can be beautiful if grounded in a shared set of data and objectives. Be comfortable with the fact that marketing expertise won't necessarily change the CEO's mind. Hit the ground running on day one because the time in the role to make an impact may be limited. Be okay with finding a new job every couple of years. Failure by external standards is inevitable.

Story 16 Takeaways:

- **Foster strong CEO relationships.** Lean into marketing best practices and be prepared to defend your decisions and performance with measurable outcomes. This is especially critical in founder-led organizations.

- **Hit the ground running.** Short tenures are common for CMOs. Get started quickly to maximize impact and achieve some fast wins.

- **Enter a startup with eyes wide open.** The average CMO tenure is often shorter than the planned exit strategy, so payout may be risky or nonexistent. Know where the company is in its planned journey (and then double the founder's timeline).

- **Develop a thick skin.** Everyone believes that marketing is easy, and they will question all of your decisions.

- **Collaborate and co-elevate.** Invest time in sales and marketing collaboration. Alignment on shared objectives and goals is critical for operational excellence and your own sanity.

Epilogue

I treasured every single moment of my glorious six-month sabbatical. What a gift it was to be able to take that time off to learn to rest, be present, and find margin to think and imagine. I was incredibly blessed and grateful that my husband was supportive of this break and that all the magic of timing for budget and benefits lined up to enable this season of life. But let's be honest, I was still an achiever who woke up with a punch list every day. Despite my best intentions at laziness, I was just not wired to "veg" on the couch all day. So, here is what I did.

1. I wrote this book (and then re-wrote it twice and finally split it into two books).
2. I ran a 5K.
3. I watched every movie nominated for a Golden Globe that year (except the ones that hadn't been released yet).
4. I went on a girls' trip to Nashville.
5. I spent the weekend in a yurt with my husband in Wimberley, TX.
6. I wandered around the Florida Keys for a week with my family.
7. I hosted a Christmas party.
8. I went to an Aggie football game. Gig 'em!
9. I ran the concession stand for my son's football team.
10. I served as videographer for my other son's football team.
11. I joined two boards, one for-profit and one nonprofit.

12. I played golf at Barton Creek Country Club with some of my favorite Christ-following business leaders.

13. I had 106 coffees, lunches, and Zoom chats with mentors, peers, friends, and new people I met through the sabbatical.

14. I read *The Hard Thing About Hard Things* by Ben Horowitz (which I highly recommend to anyone who works in business or tech), *Going There* by Katie Couric, *Paper Palace* by Miranda Cowley Heller, *Every Good Endeavor* by Tim Keller, *The Extraordinary Life of Sam Hell* by Robert Dugoni, and *The Midnight Library* by Matt Haig.

15. I watched *Yellowstone, Clickbait, Maid, White Lotus, Nine Perfect Strangers, All American, Truth be Told,* and a few others.

16. I finished all my Christmas shopping and wrapping by December 16.

17. I rebuilt my Christmas card list (well over 100) from scratch after my hard drive got fried.

18. I recorded two Podcasts.

19. I made my first cheesecake.

20. I attended over 100 football practices, basketball practices, horse lessons, gymnastics classes, and baseball tournaments for my kiddos. This was my favorite part!

21. I attended the Global Leadership Summit.

22. I grew my first two gray hairs.

It was a busy season that filled my bucket and left me ready to conquer the world. As the great Anne Lamott said, "Almost everything will work again if you unplug it for a few minutes… including you." Over those 106 coffees, the number one question I was asked was, "How do I take a sabbatical?" I guess the short answer is to "get fired" and "have a spouse with medical benefits."

Time away to reflect on my faith and how God could use my work as a mission field helped me build my confidence in the purpose-driven baseline of glorifying God through my career. I was able to view opportunities through the lens of culture, people, and integrity rather than money and title. I needed to be a part of something meaningful where I could make a significant impact. I wanted to use my brain and capabilities to grow a company, not to navigate internal bureaucracy or politics. James 1:2-4 explains, *"Consider it all joy, my brethren, when you encounter various trials, knowing that the testing of your faith produces endurance. And let endurance have its perfect result, so that you may be perfect and complete, lacking in nothing."* I believe that God uses pain to draw us closer to Him, to sanctify us as believers in Christ, and to make us more human and vulnerable to disciple others.

As I considered the return to work, I wanted to pivot and try something new. I had a very financially accretive opportunity that came along as a divisional CMO for a large, well-known enterprise. However, it was officially at the Vice President level, despite a very generous compensation package, rather than at the Senior Vice President or Chief Marketing Officer title. I struggled with this. I didn't want to care about the title, but I did because, as a representative of this executive sabbatical movement, I felt a responsibility to show the world that taking time off as a leader, especially a female leader, wouldn't (or shouldn't) penalize you or your job title. Leading with intention makes you better, more interesting, more passionate, and more purposeful. Companies should recognize and appreciate that, but a step back in title could be damaging and cause future leaders to sacrifice their own mental health and rest to protect the speed of their career progression.

I did something a little different that I may not have considered before taking a sabbatical. I joined a start-up. I received a call from Simon, the CEO and Founder of a Series A venture capital-backed Software as a Service (SaaS) company called HYCU, during my last week of work before my sabbatical. He was looking for a Chief Marketing Officer to help take HYCU to the next level and accelerate the demand engine. Simon and his contagious energy blew me away, and I was inspired by his mission to build a safer world through data protection. However, I wasn't in the right headspace to consider the opportunity. Despite my interest in the role and desire to work for Simon, I told him two things:

1. "I will never work for a founder again."
2. "I am taking a six-month sabbatical. Good luck with your search."

He was floored, but he understood my need for a break. He stayed in touch over the next few months while he continued to interview other candidates. He would email me and say things like, *"I just interviewed my 38th CMO candidate, and none of them are you."* Finally, he came back to me and offered me a chance to join HYCU as the CMO in January 2022 upon completion of my sabbatical. Simon pursued me, and that felt empowering. He assured me that he would never operate like the founder I worked for previously, that he would trust me 100% to make marketing decisions, and that he would always allow me to prioritize my family life outside of work. I was ready to jump. God laid this opportunity in front of me in His perfect time for His perfect purpose. I accepted the role and joined HYCU as their first-ever CMO in January 2022.

I did the work to know that I could trust my gut again because I settled into the reality that there was a plan for my life. What's more, I learned over time that my gut was not a static entity. What my gut might have told me today was different from what I might have felt tomorrow. I was human. My mind could change. The term "gut" was shorthand for putting my trust in the One who gave me life. To me, that meant the Holy Spirit working in my life through the power and sovereignty of the Lord Jesus Christ. So, when things changed from day to day, I had to have faith that God was in control and had a plan. He had all the facts, and He had the roadmap for His master purpose. I won't pretend to know even a fraction of the infinite horizon that God could see, so I just had to trust. I just had to listen and discern the voice that is uniquely His. I was not in control.

God had a purpose in all of it, bringing me to this very moment with all the experiences in my toolkit, the scars to show for it, and the pebbles in my pocket to last a lifetime. My journey had just begun, but it didn't happen by accident. As the legendary Dolly Parton said, "I just let go and let God lead me." Despite my best intentions to control every decision and result, God is in charge. I just needed to stay true to myself and my beliefs and be open to where God led.

Romans 8:28 says, *"And we know that for those who love God, all things work together for good, for those who are called according to his purpose."* I am seeking to listen to His purpose. Rising above the noise. Rising above other people's expectations. Rising above the limitations of my own imposter syndrome. Rising above the unrealistic, self-imposed expectations of perfection. Rising above all the pressure to say yes.

Every day, I am rising.

Acknowledgments

I have never written a book before. When I left corporate for six months to take a sabbatical, I had so many thoughts in my head that I needed to get out. My family would leave for work and school every day, and I would just sit down at the computer and write. I needed to come to terms with who I was, how I got here, and where I wanted to go moving forward. I also felt this need to tell my story in case anything ever happened to me. I wanted my kids to know who their mom was.

I started from the beginning and thought through every key milestone throughout my life—from childhood to college to career to my family. I began to notice themes, like worrying more about what others thought than what God had planned for me. Or always doing what I thought was expected of me rather than really knowing where my heart was leading. Unpacking those motivations helped me come to terms with all the decisions I have made over the last four decades.

After I wrote everything down, a content editor reviewed it to help with structure. Then, I had my mom, Patsy Vann, a retired English teacher and a fantastic writer, conduct a copy edit review to check all the grammar, tense, and sentence structure. She printed out all 250 pages, bound them in a green, three-ring binder, and marked each edit in pencil. Inside the front cover of the binder, she wrote me a note to tell me how "overly proud and amazed" she was and that this "huge undertaking" reflects exactly who I am every day. I am so grateful that my mom was able to walk this journey with me.

The original book was 70,000 words. Apparently, that is about twice as long as a normal nonfiction book. So late in the game, after incorporating all of the edits, I split the book in half and re-structured the flow and layout. The first half was all about a massive failure in my personal life that opened the most magical door to meeting Jim—my best friend, my soulmate, my husband. The second half was more professional about my journey to the C-suite and all the nuggets I learned along the way. The latter of those two manuscripts is *Rising*.

I hope you have enjoyed this book. The stories and insights would not have been possible without my incredible mentors, leaders, adversaries, and venting buddies along the way—Brett, Ellen, Al, Margaret, John, JT, Lisa, Pat, Dave, Carla, David, Rachel, Ashley, Joanna, Ken, Simon, TJ, "Tom," Kim, and a host of others. The daily balance between being a strong female executive and a present mom and wife with my kids is a constant dance, but I am so blessed by the life God planned for me and for the privilege of getting to walk through it every day. I screw it up so badly sometimes and still come out the other side with hope and gratitude. And I still have a lot of living to do, so consider this part one. In the meantime, I am rising.

Resources

Story Takeaways:

1. Believe in yourself first. Others will follow.

- **Aspire for greatness.** Dream big and take action towards making it a reality. Pursue what may seem unreachable.

- **Advocate for yourself.** No one cares more about your journey than you do. Have confidence in your abilities. Don't let limitations define your potential. Own your story.

- **Always be learning.** Broaden your skill sets and explore new fields, even if they weren't part of the original plan.

- **Trust the journey.** Know that it is part of something bigger that is beyond your imagination.

- **Embrace and appreciate differences.** Regardless of people, beliefs, and lifestyles, engage in conversations that challenge your perspectives and allow you to grow.

2. Stay open to it.

- **Just say "Yes."** Be open to it. The possibilities are more than you can imagine.

- **Cultivate authentic relationships.** They could open doors to future opportunities.

- **Trust that the timing is always perfect.** Don't dismiss opportunities too quickly. Give them a chance to unfold and reveal their potential.

- **Appreciate direct communication.** A straightforward approach leaves little chance of misinterpretation.

- **Lean into change.** While stability has its merits, being open to new challenges and ideas can introduce growth opportunities that you could have never dreamed of on your own.

3. Consumer packaged goods is the ultimate marketing training ground.

- **Be the CEO of your brand.** Consumer packaged goods allows you to understand all the levers to maximize revenue. Don't just be a marketer. Be a business athlete.

- **The power is in the numbers.** Use quantitative insights to understand market trends, defend strategies, troubleshoot issues, and secure investment from leadership.

- **Embrace a customer-first mindset.** Understand the pain points and needs of your target audience deeply and create solutions that resonate and differentiate in a crowded market.

- **There is more to marketing than advertising.** Implement comprehensive, 360° plans that address consumer challenges, increase purchase frequency, boost revenue, and enhance brand loyalty. Think about packaging, pricing, presentation, and customer delight.

4. Live in NYC at least once in your lifetime.

- **Embrace a fresh start.** New cities mean new beginnings and opportunities. Approach changes with energy and hope.

- **Inspire creativity.** The vibrant atmosphere of New York City can infuse energy into your life and fuel your personal and professional growth.

- **Face your fears head-on.** Overcome unexpected challenges in unfamiliar places with an open mind, a positive attitude, and resilience. Embrace uncertainty and discomfort as opportunities for growth.

- **Give people the benefit of the doubt.** Start with trust and kindness. People will often surprise you with a willingness to help in return.

- **Live within your means.** NYC is extremely expensive, regardless of your career or educational background. Grab five roommates, rent a 1-bedroom unit in the village, eat all of the delicious food, and spend days roaming the streets and experiencing life.

5. The degree of Imposter Syndrome depends on the audience.

- **Capitalize on a shorter learning curve.** Each experience builds on the last, reducing the time it takes to assess, triangulate, and make an impact in future roles. Write down what you learned after each experience. You'll be shocked at how worthy you are.

- **Ask for help.** Stand on the shoulders of the leaders who came before you. Seek mentorship and wisdom from their experience to help inform your approach.

171

- **Build trust.** Invest time with your new boss and leadership team before you start. By establishing command of your function early, you will inspire their confidence and trust so you can hit the ground running on day one.

- **Confidence begets confidence.** The more your team believes in you, the more you will trust yourself to make bold decisions without apology. Know your audience and level-set your expectations based on what they need from you.

- **Take time to grow in your role.** Whether it's personal or professional, leadership comes with visibility and high expectations, but you don't need to have all the answers immediately. Prioritize quality of impact over speed of execution.

6. God's plan is always perfect.

- **Leverage a career pivot strategy.** When changing careers or roles, leverage at least one existing experience as a foundation while making targeted pivots to new industries, functions, or locations. This approach can help mitigate risk and provide a smoother transition throughout your career.

- **Balance your values with practical decisions.** Evaluate situations based on both your beliefs and opportunity to ensure you are making the best life decision, not just a career choice.

- **Trust the timing and the process.** God's plan is always perfect. Even when things seem uncertain or stressful, understand that His plan is always the right one, even if it feels different from our own. We just can't see the full picture.

- **Listen to your body.** Stress and anxiety can affect you in a number of different ways. Recognize those physical and emotional effects and seek ways to manage the stress, whether through prayer, professional help, hobbies, or support from friends and family.

- **Have hope for the future.** Stay anchored in your faith and remain open to possibilities, even in uncertain times.

7. Traveling the world expands your perspective.

- **Solo travel enables self-reflection.** Exploring new places by yourself in a foreign place is an incredible means of self-reflection and growth, allowing you to process your thoughts and feelings, learn more about yourself, and gain a deeper perspective and appreciation of your life.

- **Embrace cultural diversity**. Experiencing the diverse lifestyles of the world can help you develop open-mindedness and cultural sensitivity, which are critical in today's global business environment. Don't just travel from the airport to the hotel and back. Immerse yourself in the culture.

- **Recognize your privilege.** Every part of the world might not be ready for the privileges you have become accustomed to, which means every colleague you work with might be coming from a different perspective or expectation. Embrace the differences, be flexible and tolerant, and learn to adopt quick problem-solving skills to adapt to any situation.

- **Maintain a curious mindset.** Seek out new experiences anywhere you can. Always be learning. Always be exploring. Always be living.

- **Cherish the small joys of life.** Enjoy regional foods, admire unique art and architecture, and immerse yourself in local experiences. Appreciate the little things.

8. Lateral moves develop more well-rounded leaders.

- **Leadership takes time.** Great leadership goes far beyond mastering technical or functional skills. Soft skills like developing emotional intelligence, navigating complex relationships, and mastering situational awareness require experience over time. Quick promotions do not always allow for a comprehensive understanding of leadership dynamics.

- **Gather experiences, not progressive job titles.** Recognize that lateral moves don't always result in immediate promotions, but the intangible benefits of unique experience, broader skills, and deeper understanding of the business will eventually pay off in more significant leadership opportunities.

- **Craft authentic narratives.** Learn to effectively communicate your story that highlights how each career step contributed to your unique value proposition. Focus on significant achievements or contributions that build credibility in progressing your career goals.

- **Diversify your responsibilities.** Embrace the idea that lateral moves offer a unique perspective that will yield more holistic learning and a much more versatile leadership style. The opportunity to expand your range is most prevalent at the pre-director level.

9. Find Meaning in the Suffering.

- **Embrace the suck.** God doesn't waste pain. Sometimes, things happen when you least expect them, but God's plan is always perfect. It provides you with the perspective to comfort and empathize with others who are going through similar struggles.

- **Be willing to pivot.** Industries evolve and change over time. Be willing to learn new skills to thrive in declining sectors. Your ability to embrace change can lead to resilience and success.

- **Approach layoffs with empathy, authenticity, and speed.** Treat others with the respect and consideration you would want in their situation.

- **Always be running toward something great.** When considering career moves, reflect on whether you're running toward something brilliant or away from something less desirable. Ensure your decisions are about growth aligned to your goals and values rather than just avoiding something.

- **Optimize your business for efficiency.** Minimize unnecessary costs, streamline workflows, and make tough decisions that benefit both the business and the people involved.

10. Don't be a doormat. Speak up for yourself.

- **Tackle the obstacles.** Even if situations seem challenging, confront adversity as an opportunity to learn, adapt, and come out stronger on the other side. Extract insights and knowledge from tough experiences that will help you grow professionally and personally.

- **Disconnect daily.** When considering career moves, make sure you have support at home and block significant time every day to disconnect and be completely present with your family. Seek to strike a balance between achieving your professional goals and maintaining important family values. If they are in conflict, make a change.

- **Stand up for your worth and value.** Don't be a passive participant in your career journey. Advocate for yourself, address concerns, and seek the respect you deserve. Believe in your skills and capabilities. Open, honest communication can lead to better understanding, improved relationships, and a healthier work environment.

- **Strive for mutual respect with your leaders.** Push back when necessary but do so professionally and thoughtfully. Demonstrate that you can handle challenges. Holding your ground can earn you respect.

- **Be both competent and confident.** Being capable at your job is important, but having the confidence to assert yourself, take on challenges, and communicate effectively is critical for allowing your competence to shine.

11. Joy at work can affect your leadership style.

- **Connect your work to your values.** Seek out workplace cultures that align with your beliefs and contribute to your overall well-being.

- **Embrace your strengths.** The return on your investment will be far greater than trying to fix your weaknesses. Building on your strengths will allow you to excel in the right role, leading to greater fulfillment at work and more effective leadership.

- **Adapt as your career progresses.** Your personality and leadership style will evolve over time based on your experiences and environments. Embrace your authentic self in your leadership role. Being genuine and confident in your own expertise can inspire trust and respect from your team.

- **Cultivate a diverse environment.** It's not just about ethnicity, gender, and orientation. Seek to understand different perspectives, work styles, and approaches within your team. Tailor your communication style to accommodate various personality types and create an environment where individuals feel confident sharing their full selves.

12. Speak with a period, not a question mark.

- **Speak with conviction and confidence.** Avoid using uptalk which can undermine the strength of your words. Present with gravitas and build credibility through your hard work, achievements, and performance impact.

- **Don't overcompensate for success by weakening your communication.** Present your ideas assertively. Use declarative sentences rather than turning them into questions. Avoid over-explanation by delivering your point succinctly and clearly. "No" is a complete sentence.

- **Balance collaboration and authority.** You can be a team player while also projecting confidence, approachability, and leadership in your communication.

- **Challenge stereotypes.** Don't believe everything you see on TV that may affect the way you think you are expected to behave in professional situations. Focus instead on being respected and taken seriously while being true to yourself.

13. Set boundaries and protect your non-negotiables.

- **Be crystal clear on your non-negotiables.** You might not get the job, but the alternative is worse. Sacrificing what is important to you is not worth that job. Negotiate for balance and communicate your needs confidently. Then back them up with hard work and trust building.

- **Set boundaries that align with your priorities.** And don't apologize for them. Success is not purely defined in the workplace. Put a value on the comprehensive success of career plus personal that allows the combination to thrive.

- **Keep your trust circle small.** When working on creative projects or making major life decisions, too many opinions will dilute the integrity and intent. Motivations vary from person to person, so stay true to the vision.

14. Women are a gift, even if we're a pain in the butt sometimes.

- **Support other women.** As you rise, lift others up with you. Celebrate their achievements, and contribute to a culture of collaboration and empowerment. Cherish relationships over projects or results.

- **Emulate the qualities of a Proverbs 31 woman.** Be strong, respectable, wise, kind, and humorous. Balance work, home, and personal growth. Own your position as a ladyboss while appreciating and learning from the strengths of your male and female counterparts.

- **Compartmentalize feedback.** Learn to distinguish between functional performance reviews and professional character attacks.

Everyone has development areas, but that doesn't make us unworthy.

15. Know your value. Don't apologize for it.

- **Know your worth.** Understand your value and the contribution you bring to the table. Be able to specify your key differentiation, unique value proposition, and proven impact.

- **Communicate your value, don't apologize for it.** Don't hesitate to ask for what you deserve, especially when taking on additional responsibilities. Overcome the fear of being seen as opportunistic by communicating your worth confidently.

- **Understand your definition of success.** Strive to balance worldly ambition with obedience to your values and beliefs.

- **Get the job done first.** While compensation is important, fulfilling your responsibilities and delivering value for the company takes precedence.

16. The average CMO has a short shelf life.

- **Foster strong CEO relationships.** Lean into marketing best practices and be prepared to defend your decisions and performance with measurable outcomes. This is especially critical in founder-led organizations.

- **Hit the ground running.** Short tenures are common for CMOs. Get started quickly to maximize impact and achieve some fast wins.

- **Enter a startup with eyes wide open.** The average CMO tenure is often shorter than the planned exit strategy, so payout may be risky or nonexistent. Know where the company is in its planned journey (and then double the founder's timeline).

- **Develop a thick skin.** Everyone believes that marketing is easy, and they will question all of your decisions.

- **Collaborate and co-elevate.** Invest time in sales and marketing collaboration. Alignment on shared objectives and goals is critical for operational excellence and your own sanity.

THANK YOU FOR READING MY BOOK!

CONNECT WITH ME AND DISCOVER MORE RESOURCES AND INSIGHTS. LET'S RISE TOGETHER.

Simply Scan the QR Code Here:

www.ingramcontent.com/pod-product-compliance
Lightning Source LLC
LaVergne TN
LVHW052025080426
835513LV00018B/2162